Thriving into Thirty

A 30 Things Guide
For The Growth Mindset Girl

by

AMBER YBARRA

Dedication:

This book is dedicated to every single girl showing up, against all odds and striving to be their best selves. In a world that can be cruel, continue to choose love, light, and broader perspectives.

To my parents, Mayta Garza, James Ybarra and my little brother, Jeremy, I love you.

And without question, I couldn't have prayed for better mentors. I am forever grateful for your guidance, Lari Nelson and Ted Nelson. My life shifted for the better, because of you all.

CONTENTS

INTRODUCTION

Even before my 20's I was craving knowledge into the "How do they do it" glimpse of womanhood.

Most books I read that shared tips about entering your twenties and thirties, felt very repetitive and blasé to me. It was all about eat the cake and dump the guy, chop your hair off, travel the world!

While all those things are great and totally must do's, I found myself wanting more. I was such a lone wolf, living out of a suitcase, traveling solo, blazing my own trail, and trying to make my own way in the world. I wanted to read something that hit me at my core. Something that changed the way I lived life and something that could guide me onto my "right" path. I mean, where was the how to, for making it into the Forbes 30 under 30? Granted, as I write this book, I am well over 32 years old and not a Forbes contributor yet, but darnit if I hadn't shot for the stars. I had the fire, the drive, the motivation, but where was the starting point?

The woman I wanted to become in my thirties, what would she look like? How could I possibly better myself if I only knew my perspective and my ways. Granted, I had loving parents, but as parents do, they could only teach me what they knew. They could only love me as much as they knew how to love, be loved and accept love. The truth was my wellbeing in my younger years was pretty much tempered to the thoughts, actions and behaviors of the humans that raised me.

Before I bore you about every childhood memory I can think of or chart out a detailed memoir of the rollercoaster I've experienced in life, let's skip over to my twenty-somethings. I was twenty-seven, a business owner of three years, and on the verge of escaping yet another toxic relationship. How was I going to make things different this time? How did I shut everyone out and become co-dependent? Me, relying on someone else for toxic emotional support? When did this even happen? Was this my new reality? Did my minor business success come at the cost of not being treated how I knew I should and when did accepting the façade that presented itself as love become okay? All I knew, was that this was not how being my self-looked like. There's just no way people walk around this earth, fully happy, saying, "Yay, this is it. I did it! And all I had to sacrifice was being loved the right the way". Of course, I'd eventually understand the reason you shouldn't look for that love outside yourself, but that journey I'd figure out, had so many moving parts. So many in fact, that I look back and tremble at the fact that each hard decision I made was such a crucial puzzle piece to being happy today. The not settling. The losing everything to start over again. The letting go of my ego and humbling myself till that's all I can ever be each day. All the parts.

What if I wanted to continue challenging that notion? What if, the baton that my grandmother passed to my mom that said we needed to marry young, build a family, cook all the meals because it was our duty and suck it up because that's what's best for everyone, was just not going to cut it for me?

Granted, these thoughts were mid twenty me, who grew up in the nineties. Being an entrepreneur wasn't cool, not having the next four years of college planned for yourself meant you'd probably be a failure. Social media platforms wouldn't rule this technological world until I was deep into my twenties and the thought of wanting to be autonomous, single and not married without kids by 32 was nowhere close to being looked at as Girl Power, or "Wow, look at her. Making her own choices and defining her own happiness in life". It was actually quite the opposite. And whatever the narrative was of the culture you grew up in, that impacted your life and molded you into who you are today, it serves as a purpose. But it should no longer be the excuse of why you're not thriving in life.

What if I knew my life was meant to be magnificent, but someone spilled red wine on the roadmap and now I was left to uncover all the secret paths that were once mapped out for me? It's like my soul compass really helped lead the way, but man, I would have loved to know when the metaphorical roads were flooded so I could have taken a different route.

But as reality has it, a million and one mistakes were had, lessons were learned the hard way and for over a decade I'd live this on again, off again, " I'm totally lost in life", " What's my purpose on this earth?" phase. At the time, there weren't thousands of videos on YouTube letting you know that it is a very common struggle and that people often ask themselves at different ages in life, this very question. Yet for some reason, all I can remember is how I felt. I felt like everyone else seemed to have it figured out. So why didn't I?

So, this book, is kind of written for the 21-year-old Amber that was looking for guidance and hoping she was doing life the, quote unquote, right way. The Amber that thought she was such a failure, not sure where life was going and starving for knowledge to help her make something for herself. For the girl I look back at and cringe at, how much self-sabotage she endured. To that girl, that was looking for outward attention, when she painstakingly really just needed some internal work and guidance. This is what I wish I had known.

To all those reading the words on this page now, you are here for a reason and you've taken that step to read books that will inspire and help you figure your path out.

I hope the words in this book are what you need to hear today. This book is for the growth mindset girl, who is ready to grab a hold of her life, who is starving for some real down to earth principles of being her best self and is ready to keep an open mind, do the hard work and build her own roadmap. Much love and I hope you enjoy these 30 Things.

PREFACE

There I was, speaking in monotone... I want to speak to a person. My finger kept hitting zero, as I frustratingly closed my eyes and reminded myself to breath, waiting for help to change my flight dates. Aside from the fact that I was already frustrated from being on hold with the airline company a full 42 minutes, all I could think was, this is not how I imagined it. On my 30th Birthday, I was supposed to be in London. I was supposed to be in a café, sipping lattes, glancing at red double decker busses while I people watched. Some would say, I was overreacting, but this was a huge Birthday for me. A milestone. You see, I had just landed the largest contract of my career in my business and although I was ecstatic, I was also in tears. Not the happy kind, they were " I just want to get the heck out of here" tears. Admittedly, it wasn't only the delay of my trip. Just as most breakdowns that happen, this emotional downward spiral wasn't because of the one thing but the trickling effect of many. I just couldn't bear to start my thirties the way the last few years of my twenties were.

I had only started my European backpacking plans a few weeks prior. It truly wasn't until the beginning of fall when I realized how much I needed change to find my happiness. I'd been on autopilot for two years. Wake up at 7am, hustle 10-16-hour days 7 days a week. Going out meant I wasn't serious with my career and could never be successful, I was my worst enemy really... aside from my controlling and toxic partner at the time, but all of that's for another story.

All this in between moving to three separate homes within a single year and struggling to find a place I could call home. None of it felt right. It was as if I was in another dimension backtracking my steps wondering, where is the other Amber? The one that made the right decisions? I wanted to be on her path. I swear I had taken a very wrong turn and chose right instead of left at a fork in the road that I couldn't recall.

Somewhere in between it all, I built up the courage to set a goal, plan, and get out of the circumstances that were eating me alive. I had to find myself again. I wanted to stop running away from my fears, I wanted to stop pushing them down because the pile was just as overwhelming and scary as facing them. I genuinely wanted to sit with them in the dark and give myself the emotional space to uncover them and discover something new in my world from them, but could I find the strength for that?

What helped me get off the floor and back on my feet was thinking back to all the other times I prayed through and pushed through the things I once thought would be impossible. I thought about how emotions of solace would rush over me when I dared to step into the hard decisions I knew I needed to make. The gamble of that game is, you don't realize how much courage you have until you challenge yourself. Only then do we discover the freedom in our hearts and mind that make every What If, dissipate.

I, myself, eventually got the job done, closed that major contract and found myself peacefully alone, 5,063 miles away from home. I remember waking up midflight asking me myself if I was sure that I hadn't just run away from the overbearing parts of life. If I had done that, it would have meant my life hadn't changed. It would mean, I was doing what I had always done and just moved to start a fresh slate away from the unwanted drama that I had created in my life, but it became very clear that this time was different.

As most things In life, we get what we need instead of what we want, right? The most interesting part is, If you allow yourself to see that, to see the lessons and dissect and unravel the real reasons behind the exit doors we choose in escaping our own reality, there's a discovery of the in-depth person we didn't realize we were until we're there, but getting there takes time. It takes making mistakes. It takes stepping out of our comfort zone. It takes broken hearts, misunderstandings with family, chasing the wrong and easer ways, being blind to having all the love in the world, friendships you didn't even realize you'd lost until they are gone and you don't know if you're the one that should call first.

It also takes deep vulnerability. It takes risking being made a fool when you say I love you first, and it takes an indescribable abundance of love. The kind you give, the kind you feel when you swear you weren't ready to love until it hit you in the face out of nowhere. It takes listening to your gut and learning to swallow your pride because you can always learn more.

It's figuring out how to wrap your head around your intuition, and knowing that yes, we all do have one, then figuring out how to tap into yours. It's being empathetic to those who've wished ill on you from the beginning and coming into the realization that sometimes, your heart does know better than your mind because it's all connected and starts with you.

Your choices, who you choose to be around and become. How you decide to show up, every morning you get out of bed and realize that practicing gratitude for life, isn't some smoke and mirrors positivity bullcrap. It's the fundamentals of living all the beautiful and positive ways you had missed out on until now.

You guys, I couldn't run away this time. Running away meant giving up and that's just something I wasn't willing to do. I had to take care of my business, I had to woman up and step into 30, like a version of myself I had never been before because I didn't want to sink.

What was so magical about my birthday was that most years, I felt it months before it even arrived. Birthdays were always a big deal for me. As a child it was always a huge celebration representing another year of life and recognizing how precious of a gift life was. It was realizing over and over every twelve months to your day of birth that you are that 1 in a quadrillion miracle that was put here on earth for a reason and with purpose and just as the weather changes, you can feel it in your bones, you smell change in the air. The Earth itself reminds you; with its seasons, that transformation is well on its way.

On the night of my 30th Birthday, I was not in Europe as I'd planned. Instead, I was in a beautiful dress, at an intimate dinner with my parents, my brother, and his girlfriend. I didn't throw a huge party or get huge 3 0 balloons. I hadn't even told a single friend where I made dinner reservations. I did something very different, I spent the morning in gratitude, and I spent that evening with the very people that raised me.

It was an interesting feeling. I was so full. I was right where I needed to be, and the special candles I bought, that I hoped would be placed on a French pastry, was in a wonderful American cake instead. I went home before midnight and I laid in bed feeling stronger than ever before, because I knew I had taken big leaps to change my future in the best way possible. And at 30, I was seven days away from my most adventurous overseas solo trip yet.

A secret I had yet to admit to myself while booking the trip, and maybe had something to do with the fact that the change of plans impacted me so deeply, was that this trip was initially booked as my personal Eat. Pray. Love. moment, but it quickly became so much more. From initially wanting to run away from some unresolved and un-bearing feelings, I realized I didn't need to run away from anything at all. I felt a deeper sense of self, a sense that was so new and needed positive exploration. I had surpassed every expectation set from my younger self that last year of 29. I had made moves into the fulfilled life. In this space, which can be reached at any age and time, is a space where your mind and heart connect, align, and elevate. It's almost as if you've awakened the real you that has been hidden beneath the layers of fear you let stay for too long.

The one thought that kept resurfacing in this exploration of my true self was that my trip truly embodied the woman I was becoming. Ready for new adventure, not afraid to do it alone and entering with an open heart.

Finally, there I was on New Year's Eve, checking into my first hostel in the Netherlands. The best part was, I had no plans from there. All that was definite was a return flight to the USA from Barcelona, Spain. The adventure in between was unplanned and spontaneous. It was truly, just what I needed.

I got to close my eyes and sit alone by the red and white lighthouse in the lost island of Portugal, watch tourists walk away as they exited the Eiffel Tower, ride the tube and do absolutely nothing but sit in thought as I traveled 45 minutes to Soho in London. I got so lost, exploring each countries' train and subway systems that hours were spent, simply trying to read and understand routes and enter while minding the gap and figuring which coins I needed to enter. I saw true Spanish flamenco dancing in a hidden night club in Seville and even ended my nights in Barcelona watching the most handsome Czechoslovakian man get his nipples pierced on the rooftop of my hostel; Torre Agbar Tower in the background. You just can't put a price on such awe-inspiring moments.

Some of the things I had manifested that year prior, as I fought my way back to myself, were so implanted in the core of my being and subconscious, that as the opportunity presented itself, I literally connected the dots, not realizing until much later, that my soul had been calling for it all along. I had missed some of the signs before, or more so, had ignored them.

I'm here today because I've fought for it. I'm here now because I didn't let life keep me down when I wanted to stay there. Even when I was so stubborn that I didn't want to be a burden to anyone, so I pushed everyone away even when I really needed them there to pick me back up.

As thankful as I am for any and all of the wins, it has been the failures that have given me the opportunity to face what I'm really made of.

Two years later, I could swear I'm a different person. I feel healed, elevated in my self-awareness, a 100% owner of the business I started from scratch and opening a second. Call It failure, unconventional, courageous. I'm finally done with all of the labels.

What I have learned is that no one can put a price on your time, love, successes, or failures, but you. In which case, if there was anything I'd consider to "label" myself as, it'd look something like this:

"Embodiment of Self-Love" "Loyal Friend" "An Ambitious Woman" "Stayed true to herself" "Empowered" "Impactful" "Full of Gratitude" and "A woman that Prays".

Whatever label you're holding on to, please reconsider how you talk to yourself, despite your current circumstances or past decisions. Believe me, I get it. It's all real. What you're experiencing is yours to be had and no one should make you feel bad for the way you feel.

The near-death experiences are real, the anxiety is real, the depression is real as are love and faith and healing. The comparison game will absolutely kill your soul and the strength you build through surviving those negative emotions, that's real too. As real as the love you experience, and the contentment and peace felt through the joys of life. Some moments will stand so still while you try and hold in every second and others you will try so hard to let go of and they just won't erase from your mind. They all become part of you, so in what way will you allow those moments to shape you?

Whether you're far from thirty, decades past it, or just turning it, soak in every single moment. Enjoy your life, start living it for you, be grateful and know that your current circumstances sure as heck don't define your capabilities for a brighter future. Start now, wherever you are. But especially for your special day, reflect, learn from life's lessons and continue to feed your soul.

You've got this girl! Go chase those dreams. It's time you live into your most powerful years yet.

All the Love,

#1 The Power Of Journaling

"In the journal I do not just express myself more openly than I could to any person; I create myself."
– Susan Sontag –

The most underestimated outlet you could have, is journaling. As little girls, we keep a diary and doodle our names with hearts around the name of our middle school crush. We grow into the preface of adulthood in high school and by our last few teenage years, forget what brought out our child-like happiness. We change what our goals and dreams look like, we even forget that life is supposed to be full of imagination still and that being an adult shouldn't limit our creativity, let alone make it obsolete in our daily lives. This whole idea of being a realist and taking care of business as we grow up would be fine but only if it came from a place of growth instead of paralyzing fear.

There's this odd window of time where we don't even realize we are making that transition into adulthood. In this window of transition, the truth of what we want dilutes from the fear of what we portray adulthood to look like. The dreams that once filled our hearts are replaced with a new, more cautious reality and what we fail to realize is that we created it all on our own.

We repress our feeling to some degree during this time and may even revert to gossip, lacking empathy and lashing out on others due to unresolved and repressed emotions. Who are we supposed to trust and talk to during these confusing years? We can't even admit that all of these feelings are bottled up inside because we are afraid of rejection, being made fun of or being misunderstood. Then before you know it, we're 28 years old, carrying the weight of all the decisions we've made until this very point and we are full out adulting without any clear answers of, " Is this what really makes me happy?"

The thing is, journaling, is more than writing about one day. There are no rules to journaling and this process is for no one but you. It's a print you leave in the world, that is so special and depicts much more than any one day, week, or month. Journaling leaves a trail of your digression or progression in life. You begin to see habits you never realized you had, until it's right there dated in your bright fuchsia gel pen dated 2001. Journaling also doesn't have to start with Dear Diary, but it can. It also doesn't have to be written in first person, or third person, as long as it is about the truth of your life. The truth, that matters most to you.

The strangest of AhHa moments can show up in our journals, like the fact that your relationship cycle really has, always been this way. Or that the drive, sadness, or anger… it really all came from the mean girls at school you wanted to prove wrong so badly. And that championship metal you wanted to win, it was because you felt everyone was counting on you. Like, " Wow, me? Having leadership characteristics at 15 years old". If only I saw it more clearly at the time.

Then there are moments where ink hits the paper and that experience is then out of our minds, written from pure emotion and forgotten. At least we think it is, until we read back and replay it all in our minds like a movie once revisited. Like that one experience that you never spoke about or even realized you held onto for so many years, the one that makes you swear to never call someone else such mean and cruel names, because you know exactly how horrible it made you feel and stuck with you all those years.

Journaling is what you make it. It is all of life's blessings, dreams, fears, and traumatizing experiences. Journaling is so powerful because it is in real time. It's just you, pouring out your soul on a piece of paper in words that describe what you're feeling at that moment without any judgement, or real clarity of where life is going from that day on. It is magic, it is a time machine of sorts, that when reflecting back on such a day, will teleport you right back to that moment and you can then connect the dots back to present day to make sense of it all.

I've been journaling since I was 12 years old. I literally have dozens of notebooks full of what my life was like. Every now and then, I'll reminisce, and think wow, at 15 I didn't know what my passions were? How could I have missed that? It's right here, I journaled about it almost every day. I even neglected what I loved for years and came back around to it after a full decade.

Now a days, I don't just journal about the day, but I dream and manifest it into my future.

They say it takes anywhere from 30 - 90 days of consistently practicing something to make it stick and have it become habitual. I encourage you to try this for just thirty days; I mean, it totally fits with the thirty things by thirty theme, right? And the most powerful part happens when you truthfully write out how you feel before and after that 30-90-day journaling process. This is for you girl; I challenge you to do it for yourself and I hope it serves as a habit to help you step even further into your own greatness.

Did you cry out some frustrations, did it make you angry, happy, worried, excited? Were you going through something so emotionally fulfilling that your writing or typing could barely keep up with your thoughts?

Maybe you don't know what to write about at all, and that's okay. I'm sure something happened in your day, even if that means you woke up at the same time, did all the same things and went to the same job and are dealing with the same people. Does that make you happy, melancholy, distraught? Maybe you are realizing you want more than to just exist and flow through the same routine, every single day. Maybe this acknowledgement serves as a wakeup call, to try something new.

Ya'll, journaling is your safe zone. It is your space. A space to roam free with emotion and vulnerability and words that don't have to have the correct punctuation and make sense to anyone else but you. This is where you can open your heart, your mind and be so real, without any overwhelming feelings of any judgements you're afraid to face. The beautiful thing is, there aren't any rules. It's an outlet to help you release whatever is going on in your world.

Consider this your nook. That place you go to, to vent, that can be translated in any amount of words, until you feel drained of the emotions you weren't ready to talk about, if you stop mid-sentence.

I wrote everything… from my first crush, to seemingly unattainable dreams, and heartbreaks. How I felt about my parent's divorce, the beginning of middle school, deciding I wasn't going to college because that meant staying in my home town and I would have drowned there. I wrote about my modeling career and dreams to travel. I wrote about my unhealthy body image and all the lessons I had to learn the hard way. I have smeared ink on pages that I cried on from mistakes I made that left me so disappointed in myself, I swore I would change and then did. It all made me feel so free and capable of anything.

I wasn't just writing about my life. I was learning about myself in a way you can only do when you hold yourself accountable for the decisions you make and the way you process the reality you've created. I invite you to try this for 30 days and I'd love to hear how and if, it's helped you.

What I wish I had known:

1. Journaling is therapy that can heal.
2. It's okay to share your experiences and hardships with those you trust.
3. How did I not see, what I was passionate about most? Hello, It's all in the journal.

#2 Feel Good Naked

You're just out of the shower and you're there, standing in the worse lighting of your bathroom, looking at every inch of yourself. Do you feel good naked?

There's something about this statement that makes me curious. It makes me want to explore the deeper, more private thoughts we choose to keep to ourselves around our own body image. Does feeling good naked mean needing to be tan, or at the ideal weight we've been working towards for one too many new year's resolutions? Or do we need to work on our body image programming that we've carried since middle school? Maybe we should consider reprogramming our thoughts around this subject and realize that only when we do the inner work, will we quiet our deepest insecurities. Maybe unmasking our truth in showing the scars we possess is the sexiest and bravest thing we could ever do. Then, being vulnerable enough to accept ourselves as we are, while simultaneously working to better our mindset and health.

The truth is, this conversation of body image and what it means to be beautiful can be a confrontational topic. Does this subject make you uncomfortable, do you want to shy away from it? Or when thinking of the statement, " feel good naked", you genuinely wish people could feel the amount of confidence you hold in the body that you have. The thing is, whatever language you speak or whatever part of the world you're in, we all feel some level of sacredness with our bodies and the thought of being naked, exposes the most intimate part of ourselves that almost makes it taboo to discuss openly. The sad thing is, more times than not, we skip the opportunity to celebrate the temple we live in and go straight for the shame, pity, and negative self-talk. Why is that? When will the critique and judgement and disappointment end?

Furthermore, at what age will we discover that we've had the power to love our bodies fully and completely all along. When will we get over the fact that as much as the media needs to keep shifting and showcasing all shapes, sizes, colors, abled bodies and heights, it is our resolve to shift the conversation and take our power back and stand in that power.

If we're fortunate enough, we clothe our bodies with soft or silky material and layer it with a multitude of colors and fabrics and shapes. We add color to show off or hide certain facial features, we spray layers of streak free self-tanner to mask any head to toe flaws and feel more confident with a glow, we take photos in mirrors and we share those with the world. All of this is beautiful, gratifying and exciting… until it's not. All of it, is the new normal of existing in this social media era, but where do we draw the line between unhealthy body image expectations and the reality of nourishing, loving and practicing self-acceptance for the body we've been given?

If you're reading this book and you can resonate with a time you felt insecure about your body, I challenge you to embrace those emotions now. The time you felt other people's words define your beauty or worthiness based on how you look. I want you to visualize all those words painted in bright pink and green fluorescent colors on your skin. Close your eyes and imagine the labels,

" You're too fat"

" You're too skinny"

" You're not pretty enough"

" No one will ever marry you, looking like that"

All the hurtful words that make up the negative self-talk that occupy your mind and separate you from the happiness you deserve. This is where I challenge you to shift your focus to the confidence you want to embody, and are meant to step into. To experience the confidence that you are worthy of having.

Imagine you bare, walking into the ocean and watching every single label that a stranger, acquaintance, the media, an ex-boyfriend, your own negative self-talk has ever given you and I want you to visualize and feel all of those labels wash away as you shift into space of self-love and confidence. My friend, you are now a clean slate. No label defines you and from now on, only you get to decide how you want to show up.

It's time to thank your body for everything it's able to do and live the life you want to lead. It's time to stop idolizing what we see in magazines and obsessing about what men, or other women or the media feels is beautiful. You embody beauty, just as you are now. I need you to believe that.

I need you to understand that in order for you to find the happiness and fulfillment you have in your life, you need to start appreciating and thanking your body for all that it is. Sure, set healthy goals for yourself, but make sure it's for more than just your outer appearance. Know your why. Fight for a healthier you because you want to live a long life, because you realize that your health is your wealth and because not taking care of you, means that your cup is not full. If your cup is running on empty, how could you ever show up for your kids, your partner, your dreams, your career, your life responsibilities?

*"Be Confident. Too many days are
wasted comparing ourselves to others
and wishing to be something we aren't.
Everybody has their own strengths and
weaknesses and it is only when you
accept everything you are and aren't that
you will truly succeed" – Unknown –*

When I was 15 and the tallest person in my class, I thought I had found a place I fit in when I began modeling. It was a world that didn't laugh at my height. It loved that I was a 5' 10" Hispanic girl with legs a mile long. It was my happy place until it wasn't because I quickly found that in order to be in this magical world, I needed a magical wand to keep me at a certain size that just wasn't manageable for me. I went from a straight size model; which in model lingo means fitting into a double zero up to a size 4/6. Once you hit a size 6 you were shoved full force into the plus model division, which to me at the time just meant I was fat. Although I didn't realize it at the time, the resistance to being labeled as a "plus model" meant that I turned to unhealthy ways to stay in the thin zone. These self-depreciating thoughts lead me to spend the next decade of my life obsessing over what I ate, how many times I worked out, and essentially punishing my body for not being what I considered, model worthy.

I'm sure you can see how this obsession became destructive. It didn't take long to eventually realize that being any specific category of a model, or even being a model at all wasn't what would fix the parts of me that were broken at the time. To be honest, being in the modeling world is living in the same spectrum of judgment any woman faces on a daily basis. Model or not, the scrutiny and judgement is in the office, walking in the park, working out at the gym and most definitely on the runway. What struggling with my body image and going through the path I did taught me, was that confidence is found inside ones self- first. Confidence and positive body image only exists when we exercise our mindset to do so. As much as that isn't some Albert Einstein quote and actually seems quite simple, the truth is, it's not commonly practiced. We are complex and beautiful beings, yet within those complexities when do we ask ourselves the seemingly simple questions like, "When's the last time I felt confident" ? And if you're not confident now, how do you get there?

This invisible positive body image epidemic, is something I believe to be a silent soul killer. It can brainwash us into only seeing the imperfections of ourselves and it dilutes the beauty in our spirit because of that.

So, let me ask you again, do you feel good naked?

Coming into my thirties, I have never felt more beautiful or more like myself. My confidence exists within me, even when exterior judgments are cast upon me and want to challenge that. The size I sit in is health, and the confidence I exude can only shift if I allow.

So, here's what I'll leave you with. As the beautifully imperfect humans that we are, we will have days where we feel bloated, unworthy, or plain out blah about our forever changing bodies, but the solution to keeping the confidence is simple. Recognize that to have it or not to have it, is your choice. We already know we should be working out, eating healthy balanced meals, have more vegetables than carbs, blah, blah, blah. Yet on the other hand with the plethora of fad diets out there, who knows where we should begin? It's challenging to navigate and stay true to what makes us all feel our very best, then on top of that, to remain consistent.

I wish someone had told me, it's okay to indulge, but not overindulge. I wish when someone told me when I was beautiful at that age, I believed them and said thank you. I wish I had known that I shouldn't deprive myself to such lengths that it would lessen my quality of life, because I chose that path for far too long. So, riddle me this, we know what to do, so what's stopping us from keeping these simple but difficult habits? Drink the water, stay active, moisturize, eat clean, enjoy the dessert. Do what you need to do to feel good naked and embrace the only body you'll ever have in this lifetime.

Now, write down what you love about your body, every single thing that makes you happy about it. And remember, even the models you see on the cover of your favorite magazines struggle with their body image, have cellulite, stretchmarks and indentions in places they too wish they didn't.

Start to feel good naked, now. Start appreciating your bare body in all its glory and compliment yourself more often. Learn to accept compliments from others and start dressing that beautiful body for yourself and remember that self-love and self-confidence lies within you.

What I wish I had known:

1. You only have one body. Appreciate it and know that you're so much more than how you look
2. Beauty is subjective. What's beautiful to one person, isn't to another and that doesn't make you lesser than.
3. Being healthy is top priority and starving yourself for the sake of fitting into the media's mold of beauty will cause desolation

#3 Growing Out Of Friendships Is Inevitable To Finding Your Tribe

Change is inevitable, therefore growing out of friendships and relationships is bound to happen at some point in your life, if it hasn't already. Whether you are in a small town or a major city, it is a rarity to grow and expand while maintaining the same group of friends every step of the way. And if you are someone that has, that's amazing but I'm sure you have also picked up some new ones along the way.

Afterall, there are so many scenarios for disconnecting from your friendship circle. You hyper focus on new relationships, you take an internship to a different city, or like me, you graduate high school a year ahead of your original class and move away from everyone you had known.

I feel that as long as you're leading it, life is not a one size fits all, nor is it, that all friendships fit every season of life. Being a good person in society, and living true to your values and decisions along with doing what makes you happy, that's what you should follow. Do what makes you happy and you keep doing you, girl. You know what's best for yourself more than anyone else. On the contrary, maybe you don't know what makes you happy, so you're in search for it and that's okay too. As you do this, you may have supportive friends or maybe you'll grow apart. The truth is, the ones that stay are meant to and for everyone else in the world, it's up to you to take a chance, be bold and put yourself out there so that you attract your tribe.

Finding your tribe can be a tricky thing. Sometimes we evolve and we need friends that challenge and support us. We go through phases and we have the opportunity to decide who we want to be each and every day, how we want to continue to show up and realize that the people we associate with make up the sum of who we will be. Or as Jim Rohn famously said and I do agree, " You are the average of the five people you spend the most time with".

We don't realize how influential our friends are and I wish that I sought out the empowering female friends I have now, instead of trying to fit in with groups of people that didn't have the same value systems, habits or success that I wanted. When I say success, it doesn't mean rich friends or people who had monetary gain. I mean sustainable success in their lives because of the characteristics and qualities they possessed. I wanted to be around the resilient, those that stayed so damn true to themselves that it inspired you to do the same. Those that were building beyond name brand watches and Lamborghinis but rather, building a legacy.

As a business owner, the beginning of my hustle days, (which still continue, only in a much more, "work smarter not harder" kind of way) required me to have tunnel vision focus. One in which also forced me to have very uncomfortable conversations with friends about why I couldn't attend certain get togethers. My priorities were elsewhere and at the time, that was definitely a non-negotiable. Through this process, even with the amazing friends I had in my life for years, our bond couldn't thrive with me putting my career first. Don't you just hate that? Why do we feel like we have to choose? We can have it all, can't we?

Although I feel the answer would be yes and having it all seems attainable, would the reality of that scenario look like what we imagined it to? Probably not. Leading me to this, we cannot control the actions of others, we can only communicate openly and lovingly. We can do what we know is right for our life now and only hope that the people we love will understand our reasons and give us the space, compassion and continued support we need to figure life out, on our own terms. We are, after all, the ones who will be left living with the what if's, regrets or consequences if we do or don't explore what our curiosity is calling to.

"Surround yourself with people who add value to your life. Who challenge you to be greater than you were yesterday. Who sprinkle magic into your existence, just like you do to theirs. Life isn't meant to be done alone. Find your tribe, and journey freely and loyally together."
– Alex Elle –

It was back in 2011 when I decided to leave my then amazing job as an Executive Assistant & Event Planner, to a brilliant boss because I was in a town that just didn't serve me. I was debating moving back to California or maybe back to San Antonio to see what I could make of myself there. I decided to give San Antonio a shot. Although it felt good to snag a wonderful corporate job at the time, what hurt was leaving my Mom and friends behind yet again. I was only there for about two years after being gone an entire decade traveling the world. Surely everyone would be supportive in this move.

The truth is the support and excitement were there, but out of sight out of mind. I couldn't just drive two hours for coffee with the girls, help mom run errands, or schedule dinner regularly anymore. That changed the dynamic of all my relationships, and before I realized it we had grown apart. I was starting to date someone I met at work, I was exploring the city in a new way and I wanted to do was embrace this new chapter.

You see, something I learned to understand was this, there's a difference in having friendships with girls you "hang with" and then there's your tribe. The girls that you don't see very often, that live in a different state, or even a different country, those people can sometimes impact you more than the girl friend you have regular brunch with that lives ten minutes away. The dynamic can be riveting. There's a magic in finding friends that are genuine. Friends that have signed the invisible no jealousy agreement and that share the same frequency of values, mindset, goals, and drive. They're the ones you can call when you need real support and direction. You'll know when you find them because you no longer have to pretend or watch your every word. With your tribe, you'll feel free and empowered. You'll want to share your failures because you have all confessed how human you are and that success, happiness and fulfillment doesn't require you to be perfect. You'll celebrate each other's wins, support one another when you're down and you don't even have to talk every single day because with a bond like that, every time you reconnect, you pick right back up where you left off.

How do you know when you've outgrown a friendship? It's surprisingly simple to tell. If you've outgrown a friendship, you're probably thinking of that person right now. You already have them in your mind when the question comes up because you already know but it hurts too much to admit. You shouldn't have to try so hard, they shouldn't make you feel bad when you don't want to go out for drinks because you're building your side hustle and you definitely know you've outgrown a friendship when at the end of every interaction with them you feel emotionally and mentally drained because all they do is take, without even realizing it. And lastly, it's when you no longer want to show all the parts of yourself because the trust is gone, or it no longer feels right.

What I wish I had known:

1. Just like a relationship, to grow together in friendship takes effort from each of you and should never be one-sided.
2. You shouldn't have to hide your quirks or your truth. Real friends are accepting of you, even when you agree to disagree.
3. Your tribe is out there but you shouldn't wait for them to find you. Get yourself out there and you'll attract them.

#4 But, Is It Serving You

"Note to self: Let it go"

Shall we get into the calculation of hours spent on unnecessary stress, tears and anger that turned into resentment and emotions of bitterness we just couldn't let go of? Not to say I've conquered the practice of monks and it's all gone with one inhale and exhale of my breathe, or in a 15 minute meditation but I do practice letting all the BS go and surrendering myself to a higher power. I mean, I could go crazy if I didn't, so I'm pretty happy it's working out.

One of the most important questions I've recently asked myself is, " But, is it serving me"?

Whatever I'm feeling right now, is it serving me? Right here and now I want you to pick at least one thing that you have struggled to let go of, then go a step further and ask yourself, how long have you been holding on to it? How has it effected your life, and what are you planning to do with all those negative emotions?

Maybe you're wondering what that even means and that's okay. Like I mentioned before, how did I even discover this seemingly prophetic question? To ask if something is serving you is to question the value of your thoughts, emotions, and actions, then figuring out if your life is better with or without them. To do this, we must first create an internal dialogue and ask ourselves for the truth. The truth of why something got under our skin. Why did it make us feel that way in the first place?

Once we create that dialogue we need to create inventory of *all* the things that are making us feel crummy, figure a way to release those crummy thoughts and emotions; preferably in ways that are non-self-destructive, and release them for good.

Just a few sentences ago I asked what's the one thing you're struggling to let go of. Go into your thoughts, grab that one thing, and let it stir up all of the emotions. Are you outraged, do you want to cry, is it bittersweet? Whatever it is that you're feeling now, I want you take a deep breath in, hold it for three seconds and now release it. Let go of the breath, let go of the negative emotion, and release the heavy bricks you've carried with you that read- stress, burdens, sadness, overwhelm, feeling lost. Now how does it feel? Lighter? Still struggling to fully let go still? What matters is that you're doing the work to release it.

Now, the intention for that wasn't with an expectation to let that thing go at all. The intention was to get you moving in the right direction towards releasing that bottled up emotion. Now ask yourself what being able to let go of that thing forever would look like. Maybe it looks like forgiving yourself instead of blaming, or maybe you need to write a letter to this person, as if you are going to send it, letting them know all the ways they hurt you or perhaps it's even writing that letter to yourself to forgive you.

Don't let it stop there. Grab the next one and release that too. If there's one you're stuck with and can't seem to let go of, give it some more time and acknowledge that it's a process. The real progress in this is gaining the momentum to let go of that first one, to pave a way for hope of letting go of it all, eventually. By the time you know it, it will be second nature to question whether or not certain emotions, people or environments are serving you.

Remember, you are in control of what happens next. Unfair things happen to good people and we can sit here and debate whether you feel things happen for a reason or not but all of that won't lead you to a fulfilled life.

So, I'll ask again. Is it serving you? We don't have to walk around carrying what feels like the burdens of the world. Holding onto the guy that broke our heart, thinking we would have done so much better raising ourselves than our parents did, or holding on to judgement when we don't know the full story of the people that hurt you. There are too many possibilities that something will happen to you today that will hurt, upset or disappoint you. So please remind yourself, you have the power to stop letting this control your life. You have the strength to just let it go and release it all.

What I wish I had known:

1. I had the power to release it all along.
2. Some people are just mean and that's not a reflection on you
3. Life will enrich as you choose happiness over trying to control other people or situations.

#5 Burn The Boat, Not The Bridges

"If you want to take the Island,
you need to burn the boats"
– *Tony Robbins* –

I had spent the better part of four years building a business that was thriving but in an environment that was no longer healthy for me. Facing some major decisions in my life I knew that the next step in the direction I wanted to take was going to seal the fate of my future. I began searching for answers, talking to friends and people I loved and trusted with all the parts of my life and then like any normal self-development junkie would, I got out my notebook and wrote out all the pros and cons of decision A or B. Even though I knew which direction I wanted to go, it was important for me to think about all factors of the situation. At the end of the day, my choices had to include a clear conscience and no way of looking back. If I were to go with choice A or B, one thing was clear. I'd have to go all in.

We all have those moments in life. I've talked about the fork in the road before. Sometimes it's clear that the choices we are about to make will change our lives forever and other times, it feels like we have been launched into survival mode and all we are left wondering, is can we make it through another day. There I was compounding the fact that I had left a corporate job to build an empire and now the empire had turned into a haunted house of sorts, one that I wanted to quickly run out of. Did I have the capability to build a new one, did I even want to do this considering all the details of the other counterparts that were in play? If I made this move, it had to be from a place of commitment, good judgement, and all values intact. After a few weeks of pouting about it all, I put my big girl panties on, and I made the decision. I would start fresh, build yet another business from the ground up and I'd do it with class and from scratch.

So, what is burning the boat anyway? When you burn the boat, you are leaving yourself no way of turning back and the survival of your future depends on you moving forward with no plan b in place. The interesting thing about living out this process is that the mind could shift into fight or flight mode, making your somewhat normal thoughts turn into, well you guessed it, a survival mindset. Suddenly, you feel panicked and all you can think about is yourself, your own metaphorical survival. Be that leaving a relationship, starting a business or making major moves to start a new chapter of your life, whatever that looks like for you. So, what would you do if things got tough and you had the opportunity to get ahead by lying, stealing, or cheating? Would you climb to the top gracefully with your morals intact or would the actions you take hurt others around you and give you a bad name in your life or career?

I love this concept so much because we tip toe around the things we want to do too often. We wait until we reach a particular level of security, that makes us feel just safe enough, until we allow ourselves to swim in the thought of living in the unknown. Often times, we never reach that level, because any ounce of fear could make even the highest levels of security feel unsafe. When you've burned the boat, you have ruled out any option of turning back. And if you've done this, you have to be committed to pushing through and there's a power in that.

On the flip side, because there's always a flip side, some people may experience the side effects of being overtaken by the rain clouds of envy, greed and getting to the top. My suggestion is to not be one of them. Give yourself permission to be yourself and don't lose sight of what you're capable of, but then also give yourself permission to step into the woman you know you're meant to be, and do yourself the favor of playing a fair game.

Whether you're a believer in Karma or not, it's always in your best interest to do good onto the world. Don't feel like you have to prove to anyone but yourself of your will to accomplish your vision. Now, does this mean if you break a few rules you've joined the dark side? Absolutely not, some rules were meant to be broken. Although I consider myself a rule breaker from time to time, the rules I break do not take me into the red zone. The red zone is where your dignity and moral code of ethics leave you. The red zone is not where you want to be.

So, go ahead you rebel, create your own path, draw outside the lines and step into the unknown, but don't lose sight of your end goal. I promise you, no matter how tough the journey gets, there is a way to get everything you want and to surpass every obstacle you face while being a good person, even with breaking a few rules along the way.

Can you reflect and find a time when you were put in a position to go against what you knew was right, but didn't? Why did you choose not to? Did you make a list of the consequences, did it burn a hole through your conscience even thinking about it? And if you did do something that has haunted you for years, something you weren't so proud of, are you choosing to stay and live in that and are you letting that decision define who you are? And most importantly, how are you letting that experience change you?

There's an internal success that comes from knowing, living, and choosing to stay a good human. There's also hope for you if you've made a few wrong turns but are finding yourself back on the right path. Learn from your mistakes, learn from other's mistakes and comprehend that you don't have to choose the lonely road of stepping on others to reach your greatness, whatever you choose, it's your choice and you must be willing to live with those decisions.

Now what will you be leaving behind and committing to? Are you choosing left or right as you make every decision your greatest adventure yet? Was it done with a clear conscience and are you happy with who you're becoming? Do your actions and choices reflect your fears or strengths? And with them, are you becoming the greatest version of yourself you are conspiring to be. Now go out and be courageous but remember, as courageous as it is to burn the boat, you have to be even more valiant to not burn the bridges you've built with others along the way.

What I wish I had known:

1. You are responsible for the actions you do or do not take
2. Go all in if you believe you can accomplish what you are setting out to accomplish, there will always be naysayers.
3. It's never okay to go against your values to get ahead in life

#6 Your 30'S Will Cost You The Identity Your 20'S Built

I can almost bet it's unclear to you, exactly how you've become the person you are today. How every thought, action and decision has led you to this present moment and how all of it has given you the identity you stand in now. Whether you've had an epiphany recently and are coming into this realization that your identity has or has not shifted, or you're more of a " Hey, this is just how my life is" kind of person, the truth is, shifting your identity from a growth vs fixed mindset perspective is possible and can change your life. The other truth of it is a bit more difficult because it means you have to take responsibility for all of the ways you've shown up till now. It is ultimately 100% up to you, in which ways your life changes, and in order to make that distinct decision, you have to begin owning up to each and every choice. Even if we cannot change some of the obstacles life throws our way, the beauty of choosing to own the power of choice is that you get to take your power back and find the gift in all of the lessons. You can become the person you've always dreamed of, if you can just realize that it's not too late to step into your greatness.

So what are you waiting for? Cross the line into the thrive side. Gather all of the hard lessons and sweet memories you've held onto that create the winsome smile you give, when you are reminiscing on magical moments, and use them to build your thriving thirties on. Maybe you light that fire within from the tragedies life's presented you, and you've decided you would take hold of your own fate. Whatever it is that helps push you, grab hold of it and use it to be better.

You've made it this far and life may seem to be working out. Or maybe it's more of a struggle? There could also be some type of life crisis going on behind your most recent social media post that's full of balloons, glitter, birthday cake and stylish wardrobe selections. That's where things can really get scary because on the surface, we've become accustomed to trying to keep up with the social culture of endearing highlights of our lives, but are we missing the real picture of painting out and exposing our true self, thoughts, wants and desires? So, today, I want you to claim all that you are, stand for and reconsider the direction of your life. I may be a bit bias, but so far, my thirties have been the best years of my life yet.

Whether you're on the same page and ready to rid of old bad habits or understand that this whole shifting your identity thing takes effort, I want to walk you through something that helped me get my mind right stepping into a new decade of life.

In order to shift your identity, you have to know what that even means. What do you value? What are your strengths, weaknesses, talents, passions, positive and negative traits? What do you stand for? That combination will ultimately reveal your identity. Now, to shift doesn't mean to change who you are. What it gives you is the opportunity to truly assess the positive and negatives of your lifestyle, beliefs and mindset so that you can self-actualize your potential.

As most beings, our belief system especially, is complex. It acts as a software that is the puppet master, if you will, that runs our personality and determines our behaviors. It's the narrative you swear to, that creates the reality you're living in today that is built from the most common phrases we use like, "Why do bad things always happen to me", and "My relationships always fail". It's that self-declaration that plays on a loop in our minds that we can't seem to step out of, because why would we. This is how it has always been, so how can it change?

For starters, stand up to your critical and self-sabotaging inner voice. You can't shift out of that distorted self if you continue speaking in ways that don't motivate and push you to be better. You're fat, lazy, unsuccessful, annoying. You'll never find love. Why do you keep doing that thing, it's stupid.

If only we gave ourselves more grace in our twenties. If only we realized that up until now, we have been growing and learning in our own way. Those ways may look like failures and a whole suitcase of mistakes, but if we learn from it and grow into a better version from what those lessons taught us, we can and will begin to love the many imperfections, flaws and quirks we once spoke negatively to because we will have found the true value of our being.

> "Your beliefs become your thoughts,
> Your thoughts become your words,
> your words become your actions,
> your actions become your habits,
> your habits become your values,
> your values become your destiny"
> - Mahatma Gandhi -

Secondly, it's about who you choose to spend your time with. These people influence your life in ways that impact your habits, fears, beliefs, and confidence. They are either supportive or they're not and that love, care, support or lack thereof will influence you in some way.

Do those you spend time with motivate you or drain every ounce of positive energy out of you? A good way you can test this, next time you're in their presence, is by paying attention to your body. Does it contract or is it at ease? Most times we don't even listen to the many ways our body and subconscious thoughts are speaking to us.

It's important to listen to this. It can make the difference in reaching your dream life and goals sooner rather than later, or sometimes even at all.

Thirdly, to shift your identity is going to feel so uncomfortable in the beginning. For some reason, it's not the first thing I mentioned, but it's something you'll discover and may find yourself resisting. If this happens, remember that some of the most wonderful things in life require stepping out of your comfort zone. So, don't let that un-comfortability stop you from entering into your newfound identity. Remember, the goal is to assess your life, reassess, and then adjust accordingly. Do your thoughts, habits, actions, and values align with where you desire your life to go? This may even bring up the deeper question of, " What if I don't know where I want to go"? And that's okay too. What we need to focus on is what we don't want our lives to look like and then change every bad habit that is leading us in the wrong direction.

Lastly, the secret I've held onto that I'd love to spiel now is this: You will change anyway.

You will change, you will shift, and you will grow out of and into new habits, likes, dislikes and patterns. As forever expanding beings, we may discover that resistance could be even more challenging. Wherever life has taken you up to this point, it has been full of changes. Your strength, courage, and hope has brought you this far and it will take you even further. My intention for this chapter, is to make sure you know that it's time to get your power back and start taking the actions that align with the wildest and dreamiest version of your life. You are capable of it all. You just have to shift your mindset and realize that none of your past defines who you are nor do your current circumstances. What you do now, the decisions you make next that will rebuild your newfound identity stepping into thirty, that's what matters most. What you do next and what you do now.

What I wish I had known:

1. Thirty is nowhere near, being old
2. There is a lesson bigger than any one mistake, unfortunate turn of events, or mishaps I've encountered.
3. It's never too late to get back on your right path, but you can't be afraid of the work it'll take to get there.

#7 Learn To Cook, Outside Your Comfort Zone

I t's a bit foggy in detail now, but sweet memories often fill my mind when I look at my life as a young girl in the kitchen. Growing up in a more traditional Hispanic household I remember my mom working two jobs and still getting up at 5:30am to make homemade tortillas to start us off with a good breakfast. At the time, I didn't realize what my home was lacking, what my mom showed us best was how food brought us together. Some mornings I struggled to get out of bed so early, but every single time I started to smell the aroma of these delicious and soft flour and manteca creations, I'd hop right out of bed. By the time I was in junior high, cooking was just something we did every day. My mom taught me my grandma's recipes and I eventually went on to continue making them for myself.

By the time I moved out of my parents' home to travel, I was quickly introduced to a whole new world of food. I had vegan friends, friends with gluten allergens, others just simply food conscious with a huge majority on diet fads that excluded certain food types. The main thing I learned from it all was the connection we felt and the conversations we had through the way we felt about food, talked about food, knew about food, and cooked food. Before I knew it, the heirloom recipe dishes that were once cooked daily became a cheat meal. However, one thing did remain the same. As my cooking style transformed, the use of traditional Spanish spices didn't.

Most of my soups incorporate cominos, also known as Cumin and although my Spanish rice was replaced with organic Thai jasmine rice, I still know how to make it just as good as my mothers. And the stir fry, I'll never forget the first wok my dad introduced to us as he made his famous chicken and veggie stir fry, with a Spanish touch of course. Till this day, he still won't tell me the secret spices he uses to make it and I'm pretty sure, that's because he'd rather cook it with us.

There's something so beautiful about every single step it takes to make a dish. Even though I'm far from a professional chef, I feel what you cook and what you eat says a lot about who you are. There's a story behind the aroma, the recipes, the combinations of seasonings you choose to flavor with. Does it speak to your past? Was it a discovery all on your own, through family history, blended cultures or traveling? Perhaps your cabinets and fridge stay empty often because you prefer take-out. If so, why is that for you?

Cooking outside my comfort zone showed up in my life at an early age, but what took me from curious to exploring the multitude of dishes that exist around the world came from my discoveries through my travels.

I'll never forget the night in Seville, Spain. A cab had just dropped me off at my hostel. The sun had just gone down and I was in yet another new country in my solo European travels. As soon as I entered and even before checking in, there it was. Laughter from men and women, and aromas filled the entry way space. Before I could see the beautiful blonde, Spanish speaking lady that wanted to greet and check me in, my attention was to the tall, modern sliding doors to the left of me. They were open just enough to see where the laughter had come from. There they all were... strangers filled this beautiful community kitchen, happy, laughing and cooking together.

With barely enough time to unpack before I was invited to take a ten minute walk to see traditional flamenco dancers, I rushed to lock my luggage and spent the evening at a dance bar tasting the local food. The next morning, I witnessed something that gave me the inspiration I needed to continue my journey of acquiring a worldly palette. I sat at a table large enough for a family of twenty and joined a group of strangers to make a breakfast out of the many different ingredients that sat in the hostel fridge. This breakfast was made up of the most beautiful, flavorful and worldly ingredients I had eaten, ever. As if the baguette, with poached eggs, meat and Au jus wasn't satisfying enough, the most memorable part was how quickly these strangers became friends, some who I still talk to today. Hola, Sabani.

Just as cooking has done with my family and most importantly, the food and nutritional habits I've instilled in myself as a woman. My relationship with food is like having a high school sweetheart. You're so overwhelmed with the happiness it brings, you're in utter bliss, and then you realize… stop overthinking the moment and just savor it.

> "Food is our common ground, a
> universal experience" – James Beard -

What will you grab the next time you're at the grocery store or market, what will your food say about you and who will you share this experience with? For once, be meticulous in setting the table, get out the candles and create an ambiance. Use the untouched china and gold trimmed champagne glasses, get out the crystal bowl for your pre meal salad, make the home-made sangria with fresh fruit. Do something extraordinary for yourself, your family or with friends for dinner.

Go out and support your favorite local restaurant, or just stay home and teach your siblings how to make grandmas favorite holiday dessert midsummer. It doesn't have to be everyday but explore food in different ways to make it an experience. Cook outside your comfort zone and have fun with it.

What I wish I had known:

1. Cominos is the secret ingredient to most of the dishes I love and is okay to use in other dishes besides Spanish food.

2. Mom having to drag me into the kitchen some days to help her cook, really was the best thing that could have ever happened to me

3. Having a healthy relationship with food is an important part to practicing self-care and self-love

#8 The Illusion Of Living A Lesser Life

I woke up from a dream one night, I was in a circus with laughing clowns and walls full of mirrors that made my mind spin. The mirrors were tall and surrounded me while I panicked to find my way out. This mirror maze seemed to go on for hours and the moment I thought I saw the end, there stood a sign as tall and wide as a freeway billboard. The sign read "Welcome to Adulthood. Enter with Caution". Although every detail of the dream is a blur, what I do remember is how I felt when I woke up. The feeling hit too close to home, because it really resembled what I thought of my existence during life at that time and the circus was the world I had created for myself. I was feeling, disquiet.

It all seems so funny to me now, yet at the time it felt real and life changing- because in those moments, it was. On one hand, I was racing towards success full throttle, but on the other, I was letting comparison and the fear of not accomplishing my dreams haunt me. I would do so good for months at a time and I'd find myself in a similar cycle I had already been through it seemed like. I'd fall into these weird phases of partying or relationships that didn't seem to work out, or the even longer lasting phase of them all... losing myself. It's easy to say now, that I don't feel alone in what I experienced in my past, but at the time it felt very lonely. I was trying to navigate my twenties, and I didn't know who I was half the time. Granted, I knew what I liked, wanted to become, but again... how does one get there? It was difficult to be whole in this time of my life because although I had goals, I still wasn't sure what my purpose was or where to find it. What I was sure about was that I felt like a loser. I was living in the free world after all, and with as many opportunities as there were to succeed, there seemed to be so many more opportunities to fall into bad habits that could make up the rest of my life.

I probably should have prefaced this with my truth of feeling that there is no wrong or right way to go about life. What's your truth, may not be my truth and that is okay. There are people who came from nothing and became millionaires by their own accord through hard work and resilience, people fed with a golden spoon and financially supported who still may suffer from depression, and there are people who are content with the simpler things in life, defining their own happiness. There are a million scenarios that could be played out, but the commonality I see in most are that one, we ultimately have a choice and two, not all, but most scenarios eliminate the main factor that most believe equal happiness and success, which is money. Whether you feel you were dealt a good hand or not, you are alive. And I believe that it's for a purpose only you can fulfill.

On the contrary, one absolute way to quickly spin your mind into chaos is by playing the comparison game via the wonderful land of the internet. Apps and social media are truly high in the ranks of ruling our world, but more importantly they are at the forefronts of our minds and are playing a role in how we are living our life via the perspective in which our mind views it.

There's a quote from Charles Cooley, that I heard for the first time in an interview on Impact Theory with one of my favorites, Jay Shetty. He said, "I am not what I think I am, and I am not what you think I am, I am what I think you think I am", meaning we are living in a perception within a perception outside ourselves to define ourselves. I'd love to hear what thoughts come to you from this, for me what became clear was to stop looking outside myself for the answers or through the lens of what others think I should be. Rather, to stand in who I am, unapologetically.

The better question then, to ask, is are you doing your best? Firstly, you need to define what your best looks like and the tricky part is that it could change daily. Family, children, pets that are fur babies, boyfriends, girlfriends, husbands, wife's, career, hobbies, self-care. There's so much that makes up what our life is today, but the judging factor in this should never be, about everyone else but about living a life true to you.

Let me paint the picture, you're in your own season of life doing your best, and then you grab your phone, or laptop or tablet and are sucked into the vortex that is other people's lives. Whether or not you mean to, there is a level of comparable thoughts where you may feel that you are the person living the lesser life and my hope, is that you realize it is all an illusion. And even if perfect was an option, that too would be subjective, just as beauty and happiness are.

Please just do your best, whatever that looks like for you right now and either be motivated by all the other awesome people or shut the screens off. Living your best life will not happen if you're constantly in a state of comparison and sulking the thought that the grass is greener elsewhere. Afterall, whatever you're thinking, feeling and doing now, is really all that matters. Enjoy the process of your life and lead it without feeling part of the rat race to perfection.

What is the now anyway and why are
people so insistent on us living in it?

To live in the now is to be present. It allows us to feel where both feet are planted, or where our bodies are at this very moment with no thoughts of the future or past, but being in the peak of our own awareness. When we practice this, we allow ourselves the freedom we need to embrace the person we are now. And this is a major step into living your life consciously, thus getting out of any thoughts of living a lesser life. It grounds us so deeply, that with this seemingly simple shift, we sit in gratitude and are thankful where our journey had lead us to now.

" Do something today, that your
future self with Thank you for"
-Unknown-

What I wish I had known:

1. Experiencing failures in life, doesn't make you a failure.
2. If you wait till tomorrow, you may never begin
3. Give yourself grace, your path is unique and you're on no one else's timeline.

#9 Re-Program The Meaning Of Friday

Let's be honest, this really should be in a 25 things by 25 edition. If you are entering your thirties and blacking out at a party every weekend is your idea of fun, it's time for some tough love. What are you doing with your life, friend? What is it you're trying to escape from?

With all the love in my heart and as a person who also used to live in these ways, it's just the fast track to getting nowhere.

If you are reading this book, I'm assuming it's because you want more for yourself. You are a driven human being who has so many gifts to share with the world and none of those dreams will leave your beautiful mind if you waste your precious years in the toxic mindset, that your best days start on Friday. No shame if you used to be that way and you're just now changing your ways, that's growth. What matters, is that you define what the rest of your life is going to be now and that you adjust your standards for a better future.

I say this out of love, and I say this out of tears to my younger self. I wish I could grab her and shake her and tell her, that partying or over drinking was not going to make all the childhood traumas go away. It wasn't going to heal my worries of the day or make the heartbreak of that one summer love any less painful. It wasn't going to give me stronger relationships with my friends and it definitely was not going to make me a better karaoke singer. I know well enough that if I was still her, I wouldn't be living my best life, as I am today.

I want to share how reprogramming this very thing could change the trajectory of your life. Let's start with the most basic red flags of them all, you want to escape your reality. If this is you and you can raise your hand and say, yes, I don't like where I work, the people I work with, getting up to go to a place I don't look forward to in an environment that doesn't serve me, well, congratulations. You are now becoming self-aware of whether or not the thing you are currently doing is creating happiness in your life or not. Side note: This is just one example and can be asked of anything. A relationship, friends circle, school etc…

Whatever you were just able to pin point in your life that is making you want to skip right through it, that's progress. Those 48 hours you live for, before having to face reality again, that's not the cap of your potential or sustainable for a fulfilling life.

There are so many scenarios that can come to play here. Whether it's a job, the lifestyle that you've built for yourself seems stale and uninteresting, or maybe you just love the feeling of doing nothing at all. What I know is this, if you are seeking growth in your life, if you are someone who has goals and desires more, but feels stuck, you must make your week count for more. But how am I supposed to do that, you ask? Well, of course I'm going to give you a few ideas:

> *"Time is the scarcest resource and unless it*
> *is managed, nothing else can be managed"*
> *– Peter Drucker-*

1. As counter intuitive as it sounds, give yourself a break. Any changes that you make in life are going to feel hard because the new actions you are working to set in stone and make habitual are foreign to you right now. So, work on the following, but remember to not shoot for perfection, more so to just be cognizant of how you're feeling throughout your entire week.

2. Wear the nice outfit, make plans on a Wednesday night, change up your commute to work. All of the small moments in your day will greatly impact the way you show up during your week and carry you through a brand-new outlook of your weekend.

When all that may fill your calendar is, meeting with so and so, pick up the dog from the vet, go in at 8:00am get out at 5:00pm, or whatever that looks like for you, try changing your focus and time around from the usual schedule. Add in a dinner and wine with the girls or schedule in a date with your partner on a weekday, use your lunch break to listen to a podcast and take a walk, make Sundays the designated day to do absolutely nothing but focus on a passion project. You know, the one that you don't make time for but is still calling on your heart. Really take a look at how you're utilizing the hours of your day every day, then ask yourself how you'd like to show up? Maybe if more exciting things filled up your calendar early and mid-week, you could actually reprogram how you saw your weekends.

3. Find a project you're passionate about. What is something that excites you? What have you not done in so many years that you enjoy? Something that is pure fun, with no expectations of trying to build a business around it, sell it, be judged on it, none of the things that may otherwise keep you from doing it. Find that outlet and then give yourself time to enjoy it.

What I wish I had known:

1. Putting your priorities first to better your life, isn't selfish.

2. Evolving looks different for everyone, so don't be angry with friends who don't understand why you'd rather not go out every weekend with them.

3. I wish I knew the depth of meaning, in how valuable every minute of your day actually is. Before you know it, you're a certain age asking, "Where did the time go"? And will you be happy where it was actually spent?

#10 Away With The Green-Eyed Monster

If you're over 20 and still sleep with a nightlight, hey, no judgement here. My excuse for leaving a night light on is for the scent of eucalyptus that fills my room and puts me at ease for an even better night's sleep. Plus it's more of a scented oil warmer that happens to illuminate my bedroom just perfectly. Matter of fact, I'll take it even a step further to say, the only monsters I fear are the ones that shouldn't be feared at all. Those monsters are the ones that live in our minds and try to control our mood, exacerbates our days, and leaves us in a rut of our own pity, known as jealousy and envy.

The definitive line of jealousy being something that was bad vs something that could be a driver of motivation, didn't happen for me until I was in my mid-twenties. After battling the toxic side effects that may occur, jealousy wore many masks throughout my high school years and definitely through the insecure lens I viewed life from during my modeling career. Many arguments with boyfriends, parents, friends, and myself later, I had finally grasped the fact that I was my own worst enemy.

As a child, it makes sense that what I was jealous of were things like, my dad spending more time with my younger brother, the pretty girl from school having all the things plus the guy. Ya'll this all effects the better versions of ourselves that we want to become. It holds us back in unspeakable ways and pushes us further away from our own truths. It interrupts the way we want to feel and shames us into a wakeup call, to act on what is being mirrored to us.

Going back to the basics of this conversation, the initial things we all feel jealous about has roots. This is based on emotions that were ingrained in us as children, sprinkled with the adolescent manners we were told were acceptable and then topped off with the cherry of the stories we told ourselves about our past and how the present affects us.

This wonderful and seemingly natural concoction may seem as if it's what should be our norm, but what if it wasn't? What if you challenged yourself and went against everything you ever thought you knew and questioned all the false truths in your life. What if you actually talked to your parents about the things that emotionally scarred you as a kid, that till this day you swear you've let go of, yet still make you cry alone? What if you became vulnerable enough to have open conversations with close friends or siblings about boundaries, despite how they may react?

It's hard to admit this, but for weeks on end, my 9:00 AM breakfast consisted of three full shot glasses of Vodka followed by intense two hour workouts. I had convinced myself that skinny tasted better than any kind of food could, and this was the way I would get there. Digging deeper, I allowed myself to acknowledge the fact that this ideal image of beauty was a false truth. It was something that I convinced myself was real and I was making myself ill. All of this was before our society became more vocal about healthy body image and although I agree that we still have a long way to go, there are many more role models to look up to and feel connected with, past the beautiful legends that are the Kate Moss' and Naomi Campbells of the world. Suddenly, that realization made me thankful for my hips, height and Latina curves.

So, great, I'd come into this wonderful realization... but what next?

There was a point where I realized that the route I had taken, was one in which I had to turn around. It was going to be an even longer road to the success I wanted for myself, but it had to be done. If it wasn't, my dreams wouldn't get past the malnourished body I had made work for my unrealistic expectations for my body. I was at a breaking point and I knew that all the posters on my home office wall of size double zero models had to finally be torn down. As if that wasn't hard enough, who would I be after I scraped away the identity I worked so hard to create?

Many tears released and what seemed like a decade of having the green-eyed monster devour and suck me into its comparison and jealousy blackhole, I had finally felt free. All my small daily steps had somehow manifested into this new version of me. I had worked my way back to healthy. I embraced the me that I was now, decided to love her and to be honest with the things I needed to work on, even though those things were extremely tough to face. Okay, they were more than tough, they seemed impossible to get over. But it's truly amazing what one step every single day, combined with surrounding yourself with love and support can create in your life.

I had almost convinced myself that it happened overnight. Like, I just woke up one morning and all of the jealousy and envy I had of people who seemed to live a more fortunate life than me, or other girls I'd compare my body to and become sick over, they became the very people I was happy for. I could see it from a whole other perspective that motivated me to be my own version of healthy, one that I was already on my way to creating.

With this I hope you find your courage to fight with whatever the Green-Eyed Monster looks like for you. I hope it doesn't lead you to self-destructing thoughts or actions and I hope that you grab a hold of the actual value and gold that you are.

Whatever version of jealousy you're facing, you look it in the eyes and release its power over you. It's only there to scare us and only able to rule our lives if we so allow it to.

"Stop being jealous of people
in their winning season.
You don't know what they lost
in their losing season"
-Unknown-

What I wish I had known:

1. Finding yourself jealous about certain things can lead you to what you truly desire. So when you feel this, stop and ask why.
2. Jealousy and envy can be used for good, if it's coming from a place that instills a positive drive in you.
3. Celebrating others, doesn't dim your light.

#11 Discovering Yourself, Is Understanding Your Parents As Individual People

Part I

When we were kids, we held our parent's hands to cross the street. We drank a cup of milk because the commercials convinced them our bones would be strong if we did. We ran into our parent's arms for comfort, we cried bucket loads of tears when we were sad, and only they could make us feel better. Then we become teenagers who swear to know it all. Our teenage selves then start to dissect every single reason, they're just not good enough, cool enough, or just don't "get us". We push them away, we slam doors, we talk back, we emotionally cut them deeper than we mean to, and yet all this time, we forget that they're just people, trying to figure out parenthood and life just as we are trying to figure out ours.

I'm embarrassed to say, but it was only the last few years of my twenties that I worked on my relationship with my mom and dad with this perspective in mind. The gratitude I hold in my heart, that they're still alive, they still love me and they're here for me, is warm and blankets my life with a sense of appreciation.

We only have one set of parents. Biological or not. Those people who have raised us and have helped show us the way, they deserve to be understood too.

Something I haven't told many people and a story I still change sometimes, because well, I've healed from it, is that I never would have graduated early if it wasn't for the strained relationship I had with my father. Now, before you throw me into the daddy issues pot in your mind, hear me out. The truth and narrative I had all of these years up until now, was that I was the protector. I was the adult in the home, woman of the house and my Mom was my best friend. I stood up for my mom, I yelled back at my father when he would argue with her. That was just where I had placed myself.

There are so many scary things in even admitting that. There's the shame of being that kid that talked back to her parents, the part where I openly and embarrassingly admit the dysfunction in our home and then there's also pain I can remember, feeling like I had nowhere to run because where I found my solace, also hid my demons. That internal anguish came in not trusting, in feeling as though I didn't belong, like I wasn't good enough and definitely in feeling trapped as a teen that still hadn't graduated school yet With no job, minimal money to my name waiting to open my very own bank account, I was stuck. I was in a place I didn't want to be, during that time of my life.

We lived on the west side of my small hometown. It was a very stereotypical Hispanic household. My dad had breakfast ready for him before work and a fresh dinner after. I helped with my little brother and shadowed my mom in the kitchen, laundry room and around our small 654 sq ft, 2-bedroom home in Uvalde, Tx.

If it wasn't enough, that I never had a door to my room for privacy, or that to get to the only bathroom in my home, you had to go through mine and my brothers shared room, the real embarrassment that lead to feeling of shame, came from the small town gossip that really started to make me insecure.

" Have you seen her clothes" ?

" Is she the one without a car"?

" Her parents look so young, did they have her at 13"?

"Have you seen her house? It's full of cracks. I can't believe it hasn't fallen"?

The sugar cane house they called it.
Don't throw water on it, it might fall down.

It's interesting what we choose to focus on in our pre-adult years. We each zone in on different, and in my case, you would have never thought I'd be a woman who's superpower is seeing the bright side.

We let the mean girls get the best of us, then somehow, we wish we were them. We want to get the guy, be chosen at the dance, be cool enough to invite friends over to our home or be invited. My entire existence seemed to be around fitting in and being enough, as if I wasn't already.

What I wish I had seen instead, may have enlightened me much earlier in my life. As much as I feel everything happens for a reason, I'm also deeply impacted with the clear vision of seeing my parents as the individual people they were before me. So, that begs the big questions. Who are our parents?

What did they like and dislike before they had us? What was the full and real love story behind how they met, and did they love others before? What were their dreams before they chose to give us life and raise a kid, all while they were kids themselves?

My mom gave birth to me one month before her 18th Birthday and dropped out of school to be with and raise me. My dad also decided to leave school and work harder to make money to be the man that provided for his family.

Do you know what I was doing at 18?

Yet, for years I sat and judged and imagined how I would have done it so much better.

What I didn't pay attention to, was them and how they allowed their lives to change to give me the greatest gift, life.

One of the most beautiful parts of growing up, is getting to know your parents as people. I can see where I get my artistic ways and love for writing from. Although my dad never became a Rockstar or famous song writer, he still writes me poems and songs and sends them to me. That was his passion. He loved to write, and music was his first choice of artistic expression. I am happy to say that the once desolate father daughter relationship has grown in forgiveness, understanding, and boundaries that would have never happened had I chosen to be close minded and just think of them as parents. I wouldn't have this strong bond had I kept the unrealistic expectations I had for them.

My mom on the other hand, oh her heart. We would be living on fideo, rice and beans and I still felt like nothing was lacking. We had our fights, we struggled to understand one another when I left at 17 to create a different life for myself, but they will always be home. I have traveled the world, moved to many places, seen more things than 13-year-old me had hoped for and yet, I choose to live in my home state of Texas because nothing tops being near those you love. Afterall, I had already been gone over a decade. I wasn't there for the divorce, to hug my brother when he was going through that without me, or to comfort either of my parents. I was selfishly and happily away, trying to heal my own wounds.

The beautiful thing about finding a deeper appreciation for our parents is the peace that comes from not regretting that we didn't try to understand and work to mend what may have been broken. Whatever your family dynamic looks like, whether you think you had it good, bad or feel it could have been better, stop and appreciate the roles of the humans that raised you, have played. At the end of the day, they are only human.

They may have seemed like superheroes when we were 8, then we began to see the imperfections and magnified those to fit the thought that parents should know everything. On the contrary, maybe your parents instilled fear and negativity in you. Also know that you are not them, that doesn't reflect on who you will grow to be and as I'll say again, that may truly be the best they know how to give and show their version of love.

Once we stop and try to know them better, understand their past and how their parents raised them, we can begin to accept that whether our vision of "good enough", it was their best and their best shouldn't be measured to our best.

Part II

As we should see our parents for the people they are, outside from the responsibilities we give them as parents, spending time exploring our family tree could help take an even deeper dive into where we come from on an ancestral level.

It was spring of 2006 that I became a self-proclaimed reporter, investigator extraordinaire. I set out on a mission to interview my grandparents, voice recorder in hand. Afterall, the only grandparents I was able to get to know were on my dad's side. My mother's mom had passed away when I was a child and her dad left at a young age.

A 15-minute drive down long poorly paved roads with trailer homes on either side and people riding horses out of their property that had chickens and barns with other wild life, I had finally arrived at my grandmother's home. I pulled down the tailgate of my grandfather's truck and stated, "Let's start from the beginning".

In a full hour, we laughed together, cried together, and apologized to each other for not spending enough time with one another. With 10 kids; one being my dad, and their kids who had kids who had kids, to say she was a grandma to many, was an understatement. Some of those grandkids she raised as her own and most of what I remember was that she was always in the kitchen.

All those years, how could I have thought it was about me? It was so much more than just me. In that conversation, I realized that there was this exciting new door to half of my past that I opened. I learned about how my real grandpa who was no longer in the picture had left long before I ever existed, how my grandparents had survived World War II and how they were affected by it. She pulled out the map of the 10 lots of land she purchased so she had something to pass to down to each of her kids and how she sold everything to get it. One of those pieces of land I would eventually go on to buy.

My curiosity took me to much deeper levels. Were we really only second generation in America? Then understanding that the reason my parents didn't speak much Spanish in our home was because they'd get made fun of for not speaking proper English and my mom would be damned if I couldn't speak English properly.

Once we ended our conversation, I decided to not let it stop there. I went online and took one of those DNA tests that give you a breakdown of your lineage. I was full throttle to discovering where my blood line came from.

I discovered that I am 21% Iberian, which is mostly made up of Spain and Portugal, 15% Greek, Italian, French and up to 14% Jewish with the Majority heritage being Iberian.

My eyes lit up as I tried to understand what all of this meant for me. I was well on my way to becoming an expert. In searching, I found historical facts of how in Prehistoric Iberia, civilizations were trading Mediterranean communities, or how centuries ago, the Iberian colonies and territories that had been controlled by Carthage became a province of the Roman Empire, known as Hispania, which my blood line was very highly, potentially part of. Or how my solo backpacking trip in 2018 was also fueled by the idea that my great grandmother was possibly a Sephardic Jew who may have migrated. Then realizing that even before her time, hundreds of years before that, into the Age of Discovery around 1469, when the new political entity of Espana; known as the foundation of which the modern kingdom of Spain grew, where her ancestors, settled, they also struggled to survive while migrating to and from other parts of this earth.

My fascination with my roots and undiscovered history line of my blood will always be part of what fuels my travel and cultural curiosity. To know we are more connected than we are led to believe, and that just because our parents and grandparents and great grandparents may not be around to discuss this with us, doesn't mean we cannot use the tools of technology and human efforts that we have now, to move forward, to step up and say, " now is my time to unveil some of my history and past".

To me, it's been a magical experience and continues to be a journey of discovery. It only helps me feel even closer to those who once walked this earth and gives me insight to pass on to the children I hope to have. It gives me the willingness to speak openly with them, about their roots, and how I discovered mine. This journey was one of pure curiosity into what our past can teach us. Where your feet are planted now, others have paved the way for them to be set there and that should be discovered and never forgotten.

"I wish I had realized that family history is a perishable commodity. It disappears with time, as memoires fade, and as loved ones pass on. I wish I had known that the most important aspect of family history is preserving a record of the present for the future".
– Guy Black -

What I wish I had known:

1. Meet them halfway and ask better questions
2. You may not like everything you discover, but at least it's one step closer to the truth of where you came from
3. Your parents or grandparents may not have the answers because they too were left in the dark about their history, but that could all stop with you

#12 The Hype Of The Side Hustle

First of all, in order to believe in the hype and dare to be interested in a side hustle, you need to understand what one even is. You also need to know why I would recommend you have one now and start imagining the opportunities you can begin creating for yourself through one. All gibberish set aside and to be plainly put, a side hustle is freelance work outside of your main job that provides supplemental income. Whether you're still in University, a parent, not a parent, single, an alien… or whatever excuse you feel you're about to make for yourself; just know, there's no perfect or imperfect scenario to run a successful side hustle. Some of the world's largest labels and magazines suggest that almost 60% of companies are outsourcing work to freelancers to save money, meaning you could already have the skill needed to be that freelancer. Not to mention, living in this world with never ending access to apps at our fingertips, this provides even more opportunities to people around the world, to make additional income of up to $500 - $2,000 more per month or more.

Before I graduated high school in the early 2000's, I was still trying to navigate my way from my hometown to the next largest city in San Antonio, Texas with an actual paper map. The era of google maps, Waze, or the wonderfully generated music that is available on our phones did not exist. I believe I was still in the age of Myspace and the thought of filming yourself talking about life, vulnerability, coaching online, or selling products that were already in stores, but then essentially becoming an online store, seemed farfetched. To think that just a decade later, you can self-publish your book, get picked up for a Netflix series, become a millionaire through YouTube, get the chance to talk business with Gary Vaynerchuck because you have over 50 million followers dancing on an app before you can even legally step into a casino, or that you can physically be on opposite ends of the earth and have a conversation with a person you can see, through your phone, is mind blowing.

Over 620,000 new business open every single year, over 35% of the workforce consists of freelancers, (that's over 57 million people) and each and every one of them have the potential to survive past their first year. Okay, that last one I mentioned about everyone having potential is not verified but is one that I100% believe in. Do you get where I'm going with this? Why not you? And can't we make money doing something we love so much, that it makes us questions how in the heck we are making money doing it in the first place?

To me, this all ties into our why. What do you feel your purpose is? What drives you and motivates you? And do you feel you're on your path to fulfilling your life's calling? Whatever that thing is, if you're not doing it now, making these moves and acquiring a side hustle can very well lead you on the way. The truth is, your purpose, your "why", those goals you set for yourself that you haven't even taken the time to write down, it's telling you something. It's nudging your invisible intuition strings and whispering to your mind, hey, pay attention to me!

Maybe you're happy with where you're at, and that's a beautiful thing. But even then, there are loans or tangible things that you may want that could take you another 3-5 years to get. Having a side hustle could cut that time down in half. On the other side of that, there are those who have decided to start because it aligns with their passion and purpose. It's not something to just make you money. You're starting this thing and waking up earlier or going to bed later to invest your time and energy in building this passion project into something more.

With sites like Etsy that enable us to showcase our unique craftiness, or platforms and apps that make room for us to host our very own Podcasts. We literally just have to show up, stay consistent, and invest in ourselves. . In big or small ways, we each have the latitude to place our unique abilities, perspective, and talents and shift them into a side hustle.

So, why should you begin something like this? It sure does sound like a gamble, because it is. Then again, what do you do that isn't taking a gamble on the trajectory of your life? Maybe you're damned if you do, but aren't you also damned if you don't?

When I was younger it was difficult to focus on just one thing. Stop being so A.D.D, my teacher once told me. Stop thinking you can be good at everything, they said. When really my desire was to try every single thing that my heart was calling out for. I figured, at least this way, I wouldn't regret what life would be like if I hadn't. My side hustles throughout my life so far have consisted of selling my own artwork, photography, one on one coaching, producing events, singing at piano bars, walking dogs, the list could literally go on. Even with some of the side gigs that I did to pay bills or afford fun trips to explore different parts of world and experience things that I wanted to experience, I knew which ones I wanted to do for the long haul. And whether or not some lasted longer than others, the accumulative skill and life lessons learned from that have only attributed to what I do professionally now as an entrepreneur of almost a decade.

We all have room for more joy in our lives. We all desire more than what we have right now and the beautiful part is that most of what we truly desire is not material, but rather that sweet spot that helps us break out from the mundanities in our lives and into happiness.

I'll close with this: Give yourself the opportunity to fail. I promise the failures you may think you're enduring will only work in your favor and are undoubtably better than regretting that you never tried.

What I wish I had known:

1. The hobbies I had of painting, decorating, singing, and having a certain skill; I can grow any of those things into a side hustle and/or business that produces a life changing amount of income

2. Only take in business advice from those already in the game. Everyone else is talking from a place of fear or uncertainty.

3. Give yourself time to get good at the new thing you're trying to make successful.

"Leisure is what you have to give
up now, to have the audacity
to build the life you love".
-Gary Vaynerchuck-

#13 Patience Isn't Always A Virtue And Time Doesn't Always Heal All Wounds

The transition from the end of my twenties towards my third decade of life left me somewhere in the middle of melancholy and enthusiastic. It's not so much that my twenties were ending, but more so just stuck in an *off* season that I just couldn't shake. I was seeking internal growth and the path back to a person I recognized in the mirror, unconvinced that there was a way back to anything recognizable. This was mostly because I knew that even when I returned to someone I could possibly recognize, the same me wouldn't exist. I was a forever changed and the only thing I knew for sure was that I was planning my escape out of a toxic environment and hopping into a new one, no matter how challenging the mental and emotional fight.

After two years of repressed emotions and feeling shameful of the ways I had neglected to tell my parents and loved ones about the painful years I had endured, I finally broke down. After spieling for hours and reliving the last few years deciding to finally talk and open up about it; I realized, was my first step to healing. That said, I'd love to share some things that helped me, that may help you in the process.

PATIENCE ISN'T ALWAYS A VIRTUE

"Patience is a virtue" is an old saying that goes as far back as 1360 and is originated from author William Langland. This quote has been used for years and is defined as the ability to wait for something without frustration. In this mental state, you are agreeing on delayed gratification and are making an agreement with yourself to wait quietly, without question, of how things or life in general is unraveling for you.

To this, I say no thank you (well, most of the time). To this, I dare you to question how far you are willing to take your patience and draw the line between this admirable quality and the great act of taking massive action. As much as I believe that everything happens for a reason, I also believe that we are given the power of decision making, trusting our gut feelings and if you're not a psychopath, sociopath or narcissist, you even have an amazing moral compass. With this, we have the power to conspire with the universe and play our part in creating the reality we so wish to see.

So, yes, be patient. Be patient with yourself, with other people, and with the path you're walking. But don't be patient to a fault. At some point, it is up to you to take action and go after what you want and with that, the virtue of patience will be lived out because you met it halfway.

TIME DOESN'T ALWAYS HEAL ALL WOUNDS

I was in my late twenties when I lost one of my favorite uncles. I'll never forget the heartache I experienced or the way my mom broke down in the hospital when the doctor came out to tell the family that he was gone. In that moment, none of us could catch our breath… we were in total disbelief. That ache lasted longer than I wish it had. Death has a way of making you appreciate the next breath you take and makes you reevaluate where your heart and head are at. Soon after this, I lost a friend to suicide and a few years after that I found myself trying to heal from yet another broken heart from a failed relationship.

There are so many ways in which this world can break us. And the next time I hear that time heals all wounds, I may just lose my mind. This tale is supposed to help us feel better and although I am a personally acclaimed optimist and feel that my superpower is being a positive human being, I can't shy away from this lie. Mostly because it can make us feel bad for carrying that heart ache with us for years because we haven't "gotten over it".

I heard a TED talk once, I couldn't tell you the name of the person and I'm not able to quote anything particular from this talk, but I do know the ah ha moment it gave me. It affirmed within me, that I had not gone crazy. Hearing this talk and other friends and loved ones open up about their pain gave me permission to feel my own. And so, this my friend, is so important. I wish I could extend my arms out of this book to hug you, (in a very non weird or scary movie kind of way) and just tell you that your journey through healing matters and it doesn't have to look like whatever you think it's supposed to look like.

Whatever loss, heartache, or pain you have endured, it is your experience to process. We shouldn't live with this idea to " just give it time" or feel the shame when someone questions, " It's been over 2 years". Maybe our souls will still feel the loss after our physical bodies have expired. That's how deeply I feel our emotions can run. So, I'm here to give you a nudge to keep the loss of your Mom, grandfather, uncle, spouse, child, brother, sister... the heartache from a marriage that ended in divorce or a friendship that faded. All this loss affects our hearts. It changes us forever and as much as we need to continue showing up for ourselves and loved ones, we can still live while reserving a spot in our hearts for that loss to exist in because we may never forget it and there is no promised amount of time for our wounds to heal, and that's okay too.

What I wish I had known:

1. I don't always have to be the strong one, my loved ones are there to lean on if I just lean in.
2. Patience is only good after you've given it your all, you can't just wait for life, love, things to come to you but just because you don't have it now, doesn't mean you never will.
3. There is no "normal" timetable for healing. Acknowledge it, feel it, work through it, and never give up on yourself in the process.

> " You can't always wait for the perfect
> time. Sometimes, you have to dare
> to do it because life is too short to
> wonder what could have been".
> – Unknown-

#14 Success Is An Inside Job

L et's cut right to the chase here. No matter how successful you become, the accolades you acquire, the people you feel you impress or the dollar amount in your account, you will never experience the highest level of success if you're not accomplishing the most important thing in life.... Your inner *fulfillment*. I swear by this quote.

"Success without fulfillment is failure"
– Tony Robbins –

This right here, is engraved in my soul and is what I live by. It is the epitome of what I am chasing in this life and is the very reason why I will not do anything "just for money". Sure some things seem better with a certain dollar amount attached to it, and in order to invest our precious time in anything, we should consider the time we are trading for it. In the end, as worth it as it may seem, that's just not what it's all about.

You see, I could tell you about my, I came from a small town, low income family then flourished as a female entrepreneur story or admit to you that I used to be driven to succeed so that I could prove every single person that told me I'd amount to nothing, wrong. I could also share the loneliness I felt, even though family and friends were raving about how they thought I had "made it"… when really I was at the tip of the iceberg in achieving my dreams. The truth was, I was still running from some of the biggest problems that I swear I hadn't faced, because I didn't have the time to get into it not realizing the amount of excuses that I had piled up for myself.

I couldn't pinpoint it. No one had ever asked me, Amber, what does success mean to you? Even in my mid-twenties, I allowed other people to define my success. I was told things like, " Why can't you just be happy with where you are?", or " Why can't you just appreciate what you do have", not understanding that the shame attached to these questions, would make me second guess myself. What I eventually realized was that most of the people, even with good intentions at the forefront, just didn't see what I saw at the finish line. I had to dig deep to give myself permission to both sit in gratitude and be okay with wanting more. In times like this, I did what I do best. I sat down, and wrote out all of my scary and confusing thoughts. What *does* success mean to me? Do I feel successful? What will it take for me to get there? What does it feel like? What does it look like?

What is my definition of it and what am I willing to do to get there and stay on track to it?

Discovering what success meant to me was like the hundredth time you listen to that one song, but the first time you actually comprehend it. Suddenly, the lyrics hit you and the meaning just clicks. Those lyrics are finally given life in that particular moment in time and you can't believe you had never heard it that way before. I had finally grown into myself enough, that for the first time, I was able to define success for myself, no outside opinions attached.

Now let me ask you, how do you define success and what does it mean to you? That definition you came up with, do you swear it to be your own, or is it what you think you should define it as, based on what your best friend, parents, grandparents or significant other thinks? Defining this may be scary, but just remember, it can change. It's not going to be your definition forever. It's something you can change as you evolve and become more comfortable in your own skin.

So, what does success mean to you? How often do you define it for yourself? Have you ever felt success? Describe in detail how you will feel when you reach it and promise yourself you will not give up until you are there.

It is inevitable that your definition will morph as you grow into the next level of the person you are working to become. That also means gaining success isn't so scary after all, as long as we don't resist the growth or change we feel life is calling us to do in the world. Doesn't it feel so magical already? The idea that you are on your path to success as you read this?

I will leave you with this. There is no map or special guide to the success you desire to create. It's in the way you use your time, in how you spend your days and all in the details and smaller moments that make up your day. It's in your perspective, reactions, inactions, and actions. It's in the things you devote your energy and effort to and in the environment in which you choose to place yourself in. It is in the accumulations of the positive or negative thoughts that your feed your mind and the beautiful thing is, all of that is up to you. You will see this repeated over and over again in this book, because I want it to sink in just how much of this life, you choose and create.

Now that you know what success looks like for you or have a grander idea of it, it's time to go after it. It's time to build the routines and community and self confidence in yourself to get there. Just make sure that with any bumps in the road along the way, you aren't selling yourself short of the fulfillment you deserve.

Dream big, dream often and choose your path for all the right, aligned and soul felt reasons.

What I wish I had known:

1. You can appreciate what you have now and still have goals to achieve more.

2. The people who genuinely love you, will support you even when they don't fully get your vision

3. Your vision is yours and yours alone, don't expect everyone to understand it but always look to surround yourself with those that inspire your level it.

#15 Know When It's Time To Walk Away

There's a special kind of freedom you find when you leave toxic people behind and remove yourself from toxic situations. I would even go as far to say that it ultimately is one of the biggest decisions you'll make that'll define the quality of your livelihood.

Before we get into the love and intimate relationship sector, let's chat about some of the other aspects of this. Like, when is it time to walk away from the secure job to chase your dreams?

When is it time to walk away from a friendship you feel you've outgrown or doesn't align with your current lifestyle? When is it time to walk away from any toxic situation that you're too close to and feel trapped by?

I admit, the idea of walking away from some of these things can be painful. Even thinking of this could stir up mixed emotions, but if you've already been thinking about it, maybe it's your intuition trying to point you to the truth of what your life is lacking or desiring.

What's keeping us from leaving those situations in the first place isn't that we're struggling with the decision of whether or not it's good for us. Rather, most of the challenges we face internally have to do with the fear we hold of how other people will react to our decisions and stepping into any type of uncertainty. " What will they think if I don't show up" What if he/she stops talking to me because my decision has offended them", "What if my friends or family think I'm making the wrong decision, taking this job in a different city". The scenarios are endless and the truth is, there are no guarantees in how it'll all unfold. If there's any certainty I've found comfort in, it's in the ability we have to take our power back and do what's best for us. Because then, even if we do fail, or someone doesn't agree with our choices, that's on us.

There's nothing worse than making a decision based on what other people want, so they can perceive us in the best light. That my friends, is another monetary win. So, you've satisfied everyone else this time around, but what about the bigger decisions in your life, what then? How could we all possibly keep up the life we want others to be okay with us living?

To know when it's time to walk away is actually very simple. When that initial emotion rushes over your body and gives you that first warning sign, listen to it. Listen to it loud and clear before it gets blurred with the opinions of other people or masked by the fear that will hold you back from living the life you really want.

That's the realization I wish I had come to for all of the things I knew I should have walked away from sooner. I get it, it's tricky and should never be taken lightly. I'm also a huge believer in not regretting anything in life because it has led me to where I am.

Recently I was talking to a girlfriend about the guy she's dating who won't commit to her. It's not only the issue of commitment she shared but it's also the leading on, and crossing boundaries and dating with no intention of a committed future that really had me thinking… I've been there. I've done that. It was in her situation that I saw some of the things I let stay in my own life for too long.

I wanted to give her all the tough love and shake her and say, lovely friend, what the heck are you doing wasting your time"? You just saw that he is also going on a date with that other girl…. And then I stopped myself. Knowing that she knew those facts, and that all I could do was love her and tell her, that he was not worth the unhappiness he was causing her. The thing is, only we know when a situation has run its course and only we choose when to step out of it.

It's insanity to me that most of the time, we are so caught up and in the eye of the storm, that we don't realize the destruction going on all around us. We know that certain things they said or did just don't feel right, but we let it slide anyway. Or the red flags have popped up every step of the way and yet we still manage to dismiss our feelings and rush to the excuses we make up to protect them.

If that's been you at some point, well, you have a living and breathing empathetic heart and I'm not here to tell you that's necessarily bad. What I do think is unfavorable, are the many ways we neglect the value of our time and worth by letting these things happen repeatedly, to the point of breaking us. If there's something I've learned, it's that there doesn't have to be some catastrophic thing that happens for me to leave. It just takes my intuition nudging me and feeling unaligned to look for a better choice to make.

50% of a great relationship is how you treat someone.
The other 50% is having the ability & confidence
to communicate the treatment you want in return.
– Matthew Hussey –

We all have tendencies to view the world through rose colored glasses. What I would hope for, is that you have loving friends and family that are there to comfort you when you do have your first or fifth or one hundredth walk away moment. This is one of the things that will never get better with age. Heartbreak is heartbreak. Hurt is hurt and stepping away from the comfortability of what we once knew isn't easy. Recovery isn't for the faint of heart, but this too shall heal.

I'll leave you with this, all of the best advice in the world can't do much more than influence the decisions we already want to make. Even when that influence is high, it is up to us.

There's no magic pill or secret to discovering what decisions will lead where. What I do know as a woman two years into her thirties is that no outcome could possibly disappoint me if I am the one choosing. Choosing who to love, choosing who to let in fully, choosing my path and everything that my life is made up of that I can control. Don't mistake this for the hard things in life being our choice. Rather, the cards we are dealt, we must choose from there to keep showing up as the best version of us that we possibly can. Make sure you don't lose yourself in the process, be ready to face hard things for a better life and remember all of the strength you truly have.

What I wish I had known

1. It's not about finding the man or women that are all the things you want. It's about becoming all of those things and attracting someone to match you at that level.

2. Loneliness can still be felt by being with the wrong people. Therefore, learning to function alone is the best thing you can learn to do for yourself.

3. We only think staying in an unsatisfactory situation may be as good as it gets, until we leap into uncertainty and discover that we can create something greater. Take the leap.

#16 Your Personal Style, That's What's Trending

Thankfully, I've been able to capture every single embarrassing and forthcoming style phase of my youth. They all sit on the third tier of my bookshelf thoughtfully placed in photo albums that make up the years of my life. When I say my personal style has gone from one side of the spectrum to the other, I guarantee this isn't another over exaggeration. One year, I dove straight into my gothic phase, black choker, platform shoes, Hot Topic clothes, and all after being a middle school preppy cheerleader. I used to steal my then boyfriends trench coat and held nothing back from expressing myself. Someway and somehow, I ended up crossing paths with a mentor that introduced me to the world of modeling and pageants. I didn't cross over too quickly though; I still wore my 3" spiked black leather bracelet with my fancy pageant dresses until I eventually traded that for white gold and pearls.

The interesting part for me, looking back, is that we tend to think it's just a phase. That our expression of style will shift again soon and are ready to move past it, before we ever truly embrace it.

Does working in an office mean we need to wear above ankle chic suits every day? And since when did wearing stylish jeans mean I don't take myself seriously at a meeting? To get to a place where we feel more us than ever before, will require some testing. Be bold and wear the bright colors, try lower or higher heels, don't wear heels at all for a full thirty days and instead, try matching a pair of white sneakers with a dress. There's so much beauty in finding that particular style and discovering that personal style doesn't always mean it's on trend.

You can indeed love fashion, follow fashion, and be fashionable without trying the latest and greatest runway, couture, and designer picks. To be very clear, this option is wonderful and encouraged also, but it is not the only one. What if we woke up and saw the potential in expressing every part of our world? What if I reserved one day for my boho chic self, threw on pearls with jeans and a T-shirt another and wore my favorite yoga gear to the grocery store that same weekend?

As much as I love fashion police and magazines that point out how human, even celebrities are, we aren't judged and looked at in as much detail as them or half as often as we imagine. Just as we are hyper focused on ourselves, most other people are focused on the same, themselves. All in all, I do feel our appearance matters but to me it matters because it reflects how we're choosing to show up. This isn't to get confused with being beautiful or not. I'm an advocate for everyone defining their own beauty for themselves and there's no one mold of it, but it does amaze me to see how much our fashion sense can make up a large sum of our identity. What you are wearing right now, whether it's the second day in a row for that shirt, or your favorite blouse that you picked for morning coffee with the girls, it's representing you.

I didn't realize how much of an adventure my personal style would be to me until my late twenties. This period of time was when my confidence would come and go on a weekly basis. I knew it was okay to test the waters with my wardrobe, but then one day, as I got signed in the model world, I had this realization of what I wanted my internal transformation to look like. I worked hard to remember that among all the insecurities I had, I was buying clothes to fit me and compliment me, not the other way around. It's more than a trend. It's a part of finding yourself, it's an expression of your inner self that you get to define.

So make it an experience, invite friends to join, shop online, at the malls, in thrift shops. Rearrange your closet to match things you never have before and just enjoy the process. Work on creating your best self, first. One that aligns all the parts of you. Get creative, take risks, try things out of your comfort colors and styles.

The main thing to remember is to let your personal style reflect all of the wonderful, unique, well rounded qualities that make up, you. Once you do this, that level of confidence you wish you had, will appear all on its own.

What I wish I had known:

1. It's okay to experiment with your look. Your 8th grade self, 22-year-old self or 27-year-old self shouldn't all be the same look anyway.
2. Don't dress to impress. Dress as the most authentic outer expression of you.
3. Find the one thing you feel confident in that can make you stand out. For me, it's statement necklaces, statement earrings or a bold lip.

#17 We Are All A Work In Progress

I call BS to any expert of life. There are always experts on parts of it, but none of which would dare to claim to have figured it all out. In fact, even the geniuses of our generation are full of curiosity and wander. That statement to me is so vital because who are we to think we have the final plan of our lives at eighteen-years-old, twenty-eight, or even fifty? Well, I'm not here to lecture, in fact, quite the opposite. I want to invite you to the party I wish I were invited to. The one where you give yourself permission to really feel at peace with where you're at in life now. To know that even if you feel the last five years were "wasted" on a bad relationship, or you've been suffering a depression that you've managed to hide from everyone for far too long, or maybe you're just feeling like you're behind in life compared to everyone else. Whatever the situation may be, I hope you find peace in knowing that we're all in that same boat, just in different versions of it.

*"You are allowed to be both a masterpiece
and a work in progress, simultaneously".*
-Sophia Bush-

It's important to have goals, it's great to aspire to become things you never imagined just five years ago, because life will do that to you. It's okay to give yourself permission to also want that one thing, and work hard to get it. Even when; for a split second, it feels like we have life finally figured out and we're sitting in awe of those moments, we're already on to the next goal.

We are all working to do our best, aren't we? You see, although we know we should all be progressing, we keep going against the current of change. We want to fight change so bad that we sometimes fail to realize how quickly life changes on us anyway.

If we're lucky and we finally decide we want to embrace this change, what may turn us off is the work that would need to be put in to create it. The funny thing is, even when we get the job, land the gig, pass the certification, and experience that first stage of bliss, we think we're done. How could that ever be, if we're forever changing, forever growing, forever expanding our minds and transitioning into this space of limitless love, vision, power and a positive state of being.

In other seasons of life, change doesn't feel like a bold action, or embracing anything at all. Sometimes merely holding ourselves together is all we're able to give. The scariest parts of being a work in progress is the potential it has to clash with our self-worth. It can make us wonder when it'll all make sense, if ever it will and if there's such a thing as reaching our highest potential and then staying at the top of that mountain.

" And if today, all you did was
hold yourself together,
I'm proud of you"
-unknown-

As for the beautiful parts to discover in being a work in progress; is that the opportunities, once embraced, are nearly limitless. How boring would it be, to finally have everything you ever wanted and stay there? What if, because you couldn't see past that, you're actually missing out on the best years of your life.

All of the unplanned, unexpected glorious moments. All of the sadness that keeps us on our toes to enhance the happy we do experience, and the changes given to us, because we're never actually finished, till our souls have left this body.

With all the variables that can create fear or peace within us, what I hold near in my work in progress journey, are the unforeseen failures that we must learn to build on and learn from. It's in some of our most uncertain moments that we should hold on to our faith, our hope and catch those rays of sunshine. If we do it just right, this forever expanding life and our work in progress moments, could each be an experience of a lifetime.

What I wish I had known:

1. It's okay to not have it all figured out.
2. Stop focusing on everyone else's progress, we all have winning and learning seasons.
3. Don't forget to enjoy the process

#18 Rejection: May It Fuel You, Not Create Fear In You

Rejection isn't just the guy you like turning you down, it isn't just the time you didn't make the cut during that audition or being picked last on the sports team. Rejection is made up of every dagger of dismissal that has been thrown at you, and given in a multitude of ways that cut deep and can destroy your self-esteem in the process. It's the cherry on top of the negative, emotional cognitive cake. Doesn't sound very yummy, does it?

What if I told you that the inevitable is, that rejection will exist on every page of your life and that it's a good thing. Would you think I was crazy? Let me explain. One of the most prestigious actresses of our time once auditioned for a role in a major film titled, King Kong. There's this unedited photo of a beautiful woman riding the subway with a smile on her face and underneath this image, reads the following:

"This was me on my way home from
an audition for King Kong where I was
told I was too "ugly" for the part. This
was a pivotal moment for me. This one
rogue opinion could derail my dreams
of becoming an actress or force me
to pull myself up by the boot straps
and believe in myself. I took a deep
breath and said, " I'm sorry you think
I'm too ugly for your film but you're
just one opinion in a sea of thousands
and I'm off to find the kinder tide.
Today I have 18 Academy Awards."
-Meryl L. Streep-

This shared statement has rocked my world ever
since. It actually still brings happy tears to my eyes because
it never fails to reignite this flame of catharsis. This quote
is everything. There will be people who feel we are merely
taking up unnecessary space in the world, who don't agree
with a single thought we express and even shame us for
our existence. This harsh reality can be debilitating if you
allow. Instead, I challenge you to see beyond the negativity
of the schoolmates that stole your happy, the people at work
that smile to your face but talk behind your back, your best
friends boyfriend's friend, that made a snide remark about
your wardrobe, the person that told you you'd never make
it as a model, or the school teacher that swore you off for

failure because your creative mind had trouble focusing in Algebra class. There is rejection everywhere, but for this to hold space in your heart is your choice.

I feel like rejection has had such a negative connotation to it because most people describe it as something to be afraid of. What if we decided to invite and accept it instead? What if rejection fueled us instead of instilled fear in us. Allowing us to trust that the Universe, God, whomever you believe in, has a different and better plan instead and this rejection moment, was actually instilled in your favor to protect you and guide you to kinder tides. Like the amazing moments you've had in your life up till this point, could you ever have thought them all up on your own or has life seemed to surprise you? Continue to trust in the process and continually work towards your grander vision of life but don't allow not one person's rejection to strip away your happiness, confidence or bubbly spirit.

The next time someone rejects you, remember you get to decide what to do with it. I hope that whatever decision you make, your future self, thanks you for it.

What I Wish I Had Known:

1. Rejection is never personal
2. You are not a one size fits all, and that's what makes you unique.
3. Rejection could actually be your protection.

#*19* It's Time To Reinvent Yourself

The notion of reinventing myself came at a young age. It was more than transitioning out of junior high to high school, high school to college or college to the real world. I've explored many sides to myself and found some that I will most definitely never be returning to. Either way, these self-discoveries of who I was in grade five, ten, or turning twenty-five, proved to show me how much I needed it. Reinventing myself didn't necessarily mean that I'd change who I was, more so it was the redirection of focus and how I'd express that as the new and improved me.

Reinventing yourself is so much more than a new haircut, piercing, or new place to call home. All of those outward changes are just a biproduct of the growth you're having on the inside and is more so, an endless way of self-discovery and transition. Afterall, we are in constant change and forever growing. If we're not growing, then we're choosing to stay stuck. We're literally handing over the fate of our future and choosing to merely exist in a world we could be living in. This whole reinventing thing, it can sound scary. It can sound like some major milestone in life that we should prepare for, buy balloons, cake, champagne and super fancy invitations showcasing a gigantic R shaped balloon. One in which we will hold and scream, " Woohoo, I've done it! I've reinvented myself". It could feel like that on the inside, but to reinvent yourself may be something you've already done without even recognizing or celebrating it at all. That is what making progress in your life is, after all. It's forward or onward movement towards new horizons. And for a growth mindset girl, that destination is to your best self yet.

Here are some ways you can reinvent yourself, when you should and if you already have, what that next cycle could look like.

Ways you can reinvent yourself:

Where focus goes, energy flows. We may have heard this many times, yet is it possible that while we say this, it just isn't clicking? In order for it to click, we must be cognizant of where our focus lies and if we're backing that up with the energy to put that into motion. This is so important because it helps us stay away from negative self-talk and feeds into positive possibilities instead. So, when we are on the brink of this transition and inner change, we instead remember why we can, why we want to, and the core of our why's in the first place.

Another way to reinvent yourself is to assess then reassess your life now. What negative coping mechanisms have you been relying on to get you through stressful times and which are you willing to drop now, so that you can make room for more of the positive habits? And lastly, I highly recommend you purge the clutter. Purge the mental clutter, the emotional clutter, the physical clutter, purge it all. Make room for all the new, fresh, and positively beaming ways you are going to choose to show up for yourself. All those ways will become clear as you remove the white space in your life. Things like getting rid of old clothes, pieces of jewelry that you've never worn, even donating some of the books you once read to get over or move through a particular period of your life. If it has served its purpose, or maybe no longer has a purpose, it may be time to move on, rid of it and carry the lessons it brought you.

When should you reinvent yourself?

Some people call it, feeling stuck. Others feel as though they've hit a plateau, or are just tired of feeling anxious, stressed, sad and other ways our body speaks to us. It's important to not ignore those physiological signs, it's our body trying to give us a nudge for change and that nudge should be heard loud and clear. Maybe none of those are resonating with you or maybe all of them are. Here's the thing, reinvention isn't only for the Madonna's or Bob Dylan's of the world and as mentioned earlier in this chapter, the physical change that can come with this is merely the biproduct.

If we are lucky enough, life is a long winding road. The majority of us are space years apart from the girl we were in junior high, let alone the woman we're continually molding ourselves into. To be ready for change, is a time to reinvent yourself. Seeking that change in ourselves and our place in the world requires a commitment to develop beyond our external successes. It requires an expansion of our identity and redefining what our authentic selves are in this phase of life and then choosing to expose it. If any part of this section is giving you butterflies and lighting you up. If you're literally about to close the book now and go work on reinventing yourself, I'm pretty sure there's no more of a clear sign that it's time. Not to worry though, if your heart is trying to tell you it's time in more subtle ways, listen to that too. It could look like walking your dog in the evenings to process your day and incorporate different, healthier habits and is a lot less scary than most make it out to be. The trick is to go at your own pace, one step at a time. Move from one small thing, to another and once it starts to feel like you're gaining traction, step into bigger action. Much less scary to think of it that way, yea?

I just went through this, what's the next cycle?

Maybe this particular cycle is not yet complete. If you've been working on reinventing yourself and still feel stuck, this may be the time to go back to the how, the why and refocus. Sometimes we feel we need and want that change so bad. Other times, life is changing so quickly for us, that we feel forced into the same cycles, or jump on the change train and call it a reinvention voyage. Either way, you may feel like you've had enough change for a while, but maybe a certain aspect of your life still makes you feel stuck and needs hyper focused attention. When this has happened in my life, I remember that change not only takes time, action and consistency but to prevent getting overwhelmed by it all, requires what we touched on earlier… taking it one step at a time.

I promise you, once you create the momentum needed, once you sit with yourself and ask the really tough questions about what might be missing in your life and where you want to be, you will be well on your way to creating the 2.0 version of yourself that you desire to become.

> *"Life isn't about finding yourself.*
> *Life is about creating yourself"*
> *– George Bernard Shaw –*

What I wish I had known:

1. I don't have to know exactly who I want to be. I just have to be ready to step into the habits, thoughts and actions of a better me.
2. You'll never be happy if you keep working for the validation of others. Let this be for you.
3. There is no cap on how many times one gets to reinvent themselves.

#20 Fall In Love With Yourself, First.

The love we spread to others is mirrored by the love we first give ourselves. You will know a person in pain, because there is no love to share. We cannot give what we don't have and sometimes we confuse and mistake that as a bad thing. Sometimes people just can't give us what we want, and those expectations can easily lead to heartbreak, pain, and suffering if we don't hold enough space within ourselves to realize... it's not always about us.

Speaking of holding space for love; isn't it interesting that we always make room to love others, yet we somehow can't sit alone and receive it? We experience these high and low tides, we take risks, we feel ourselves falling and we are uninhibited in these moments. We allow ourselves to free fall in love with no guarantee we won't come back broken.

We fight through difficult times for this thing called Love. We give everything we have in the name of love. We even put those we love before ourselves without hesitation. So, I beg to ask the questions, why can't it be us, to whom we surrender to? Why must we deprive ourselves of the very thing we are able to give so freely to other people.

If we just learned to fall in love with us, at every stage of us, we could see a different, happier, lighter, and more glowing us.

I pride myself on being a good friend and feel good lifting them up when I know they're having a bad day. I shoot them a text to remind them of how amazing they are. I'll go out of my way, cancel appointments, and make the time. But to do this for myself? It feels like too much, how selfish of me.

We stand in the mirror and criticize our bodies after gaining depression weight. We call ourselves stupid under our own breath when we don't get the job or mess up at work. We do things we're ashamed to say out loud sometimes, because how could it be possible that we put ourselves last and more importantly, how sustainable is that before we come crashing down into a depression and on empty.

You deserve to be loved, by yourself.

Take that free fall for you. Ask your body what it needs today. How does it feel emotionally, mentally, physically? Tell yourself that you've got this because you're a Rockstar! Unveil your deepest darkest secrets to you. Get them out of your mind and start chipping away at the lies of negative thoughts.

Can you look back and reflect on the dedication and time you spent to grow the last love you felt with another person? Of course you can. It didn't happen in a day, nor did it happen in a month. You were there day after day, showing up to shower the person you love with love.

Make a list of all the things you do for them, and then, do them for you.

Fall in love with yourself in ways that challenge you to discover more of the passions you lost and don't put any limitations on this.

It takes time to heal, it takes recognizing what you need right now to feel better and then doing those things, even if they're difficult. The sooner you learn to love yourself, the sooner you will open up to accept the best kind of love from your partner, friends, parents, family, children, or your fur baby.

Lastly, learn how to be alone. The older I got the more I realized that I was that person that couldn't be alone. I would jump from one relationship to the next, or I was living with friends, always out and about. All of that changed when I realized how much healing I needed from my own past traumas. Once I forced myself to be alone. To live alone. To travel alone. The gift was finding more of myself. I realized parts of me that I didn't like. Parts that I used as defense mechanisms to create a false safety net and parts that I knew I wanted to change. I had gone so many years not being loved the right way, but I had never stopped to realize that it was the only way I knew. And that realization wouldn't have ever happened if I didn't take time for me.

Now that I know how to be alone, It's that much easier to tap into my self-care. Whether I'm in a relationship or experiencing a stressful time, I no longer seek opinions outside myself, rather, I go inward first. Allowing myself to feel all the feelings, and then backing it up with the courage to share those feelings if others are involved. What this has helped me learn is how to still enjoy hearing the thoughts of those I love and respect, but not have it change the direction I want to go. It's taught me that perspective is always a good thing, but it's still my choice and at the end of the day, I know what is right for me in the long run.

None of this needs to happen tomorrow. It may take months or years to love yourself how you deserve to be loved, but that's the blessing of the life we're given. We get opportunity after opportunity to love and care for ourselves a little more each day if we so choose. And it all starts with falling in love with yourself first.

" To love yourself, is a never ending
journey" -Oprah Winfrey-

This journey we're on now is a major one. Some days we want the day to just end already. Other weeks we wish that time could stop, or at least slow down. Whatever season you're in and whatever phase of life you're living, " to love yourself is a never ending journey".

The way you loved yourself out of a toxic relationship, isn't the way you'll need to love yourself as you start a new venture. The way you love yourself after a traumatic event won't be the way you need to love yourself when someone you love has passed away. And the way you are loving yourself now, to the very best of your ability, isn't the way you'll need to be loved next year. Be kind to yourself, but don't ever give up on the process of loving yourself first.

What I wish I had known:

1. You can still feel lonely surrounded by the wrong people and you can still feel whole, being alone.
2. A relationship will not give you the wholeness you seek. You've got to turn inward for that.
3. Don't rush it, who cares what society says. Take your time letting someone into your life and heart.

#21 Stop With The Hand Me Downs

The first full priced larger in-home item I ever purchased was a brown suede and leather sectional. It was spacious, comfortable and the most beautiful piece of furniture I had ever seen. Not only did it come with an ottoman, but they hand delivered it right to my doorstep.

Coming from a person siding on the opinion of; things don't make you happy, experiences do, let me tell you why I believe investing in new things in your home for the first time will.

This may seem like an oxymoron but hear me out. The things in your living space are what make up the quality of the experience you have, in what should be your safe haven. Whether you have parents that have been able to help you furnish your living space or you have insanely generous friends that gave you the things that make your home comfortably liveable, there's absolutely no feeling that can replace the one you have when you are investing in your own things, for the space you currently call home.

I truly believe a home can be created anywhere, with anyone. Its permanence can be a month, a year or a lifetime. But this sacred space that we come into and rely on for a rather large portion of our happiness, the impact of the surroundings in it and the tone we create with those people and things can sometimes be taken too lightly.

When we choose to pay attention to how we fill this space, it can create positive, impactful memories. Although there's absolutely nothing wrong with loving the eight year old baking dish your mom gave you that you religiously make your favorite homemade lasagna in, complete with the family recipe. Just know, that not all things are meant to be kept that were passed on to you. We can become too reliant on this and it could actually keep us from committing to the exact adulthood we're trying to enter. We want to be taken seriously and grow into our dream lives, yet we would still rather buy designer belts, purses, shoes and the latest phone than investing in a savings account for a down payment on a home or to create a workspace corner that could turn our side hustle into a full time business. We even shy away from spending a thousand dollars on furniture that tells the story of the home we want so badly to create because we've talked ourselves into the lie that we can't afford it or aren't ready to invest in that way.

So, stop with the hand me downs on everything, especially in your home. The size or amount isn't what matters, it's about what you are choosing to invest in that does. It's about being responsible for the bar you set in the quality of life you wish to create. It's about our search for happiness in not just acquiring things but making an experience of the things we acquire.

You deserve to enjoy the full experience of your first _____ purchase. And for that, I say... go out and do it. One spatula, cooking pan, sofa and headboard at a time. These investments mean something and tell the story you're building your adulthood on. Now insert whatever thing you've been wanting to invest in for yourself above and start saving and taking action to make that happen. I can't wait for you to experience the feeling of doing so.

> " Great things are not done by
> impulse, but by a series of small
> things brought together"
> -Vincent Van Gogh

What I wish I had known:

1. Don't be ashamed to start small
2. I promise it's all a mindset. Change your money mindset thoughts and it'll change your life.
3. Be grateful for the hand me downs but know when to move on.

#22 If Travel Was A Love Language, It'd Be Mine

I'm not sure I've actually mentioned a favorite chapter in this book.

Firstly, why would I even say such a thing, I'm the one writing it. Well, I hope you all feel how personal this chapter is to me. This isn't only about all of the things I wish I knew nor are they thirty things I just whipped together to share with you. This book is like a look into my journal that I decided to share with the world. It encapsulates all my life knowledge to this point, combined with personal stories from moments in my life of travel, growth and non-sense.

Most of the profound things that have happened to me, happened while traveling. Therefore, I ask you, please, Gary Chapman, add this love language and make it a sixth. I have a feeling it may speak to many.

If travel were a love language, it would be mine. Traveling, especially solo, can be one of the scariest adventures you set out on, but to say it's worth it just doesn't match the significance this experience can hold.

You literally could have been sitting beside me on the plane, landing in the same country, or even walking alongside me to some of the most amazing sites on earth and our experiences could be polar opposite. That's only one of the beauties of getting to know yourself better through travel. The experience resonates differently for everyone.

Traveling is a lot like being in love. The beauty is so intensified because, it is in the eye of the beholder. Our rose-colored glasses are on, it's new, exhilarating and can be petrifying. It's in the experience that you yourself have with the energy of each place you set your feet that could change your whole world.

A massive change that I never realized until I was in my late twenties and into my thirties, was the reasons I traveled and how that changed over time.

The simplistic breakdown of this, without creating an entirely different book to explain it, goes a little something like this:

12-years-old: " If only I could see the Big Apple. All my dreams would come true if I could just visit New York City"

16: " I'm going to prove everyone wrong and really make something of myself. I'll travel the world and pave my own way".

19: " I want to escape this place"

24: " What if I miss the best years of my young adulthood with family? They need me, I should move back to my hometown"

27: " It's time to shed this old identity and be the woman I know I'm meant to be. I can't wait to travel abroad for long periods of time again. Where to next and who's coming with me?"

30: " I love having Texas as my home base, but can't wait for my next adventure to a new country".

> "Traveling leaves you speechless,
> then turns you into a storyteller"
> -Ibn Battuta-

Travel has always been in my heart. I can't fully explain where the initial longing came from, but I can say that it's been a lifelong goal that keeps expanding. From the sound of an engine of a plane ready for take-off, to busy airports and new books in the stands of the waiting area. Even my people watching skills are enhanced. To even begin to imagine where each person has come from, is this their home, are they thousands of miles away from it, who are they with, what is their story? I am still just as in love with every single part.

Whether I've just landed in Jerusalem, Italy, South America, Canada or another beautiful state in the USA, I believe us travelers are all in search of the same thing. We all want to experience the beauty this earth holds, we want to connect on a global level, and we want to feel free enough to adventure out on all of these things as part of our own soul expansion and growth.

For me, it has been *the* most important pieces of my life puzzle. It was the key factor in building my character, stirring a fiery passion for my most creative self, and helped me value the life, home, family, and community I grew up in even more.

Travel connected my love for art, music, books, movies and the understanding of people and different cultures to a level of ineffability. It helped me heal, it made me a kinder human, it taught me a deeper level of compassion, it sometimes made me unsettled, until it registered that danger and evil can really be anywhere. So why let fear steal my greater desires to travel outside of what I know?

And the ocean, whatever ocean you've seen and smelled and experienced, it won't be as remarkable as the waves you see crashing onto the rocks in high tide, coming up to hit your feet when they're on the opposite side of the world. When you're surrounded by people who are speaking a different language in a country you're discovering for the first time. Even the cute couples I once mocked, became the thing I longed for in my heart because love never looked more beautiful. I've found myself in awe of couples bickering outside a café in Lisbon, and practically cried when rain drops hit my face while wondering down the streets of Paris alone. Every corner becomes magic and every moment keeps you present.

What I wish I had known:

1. You don't have to be rich to travel (major misconception when I was younger).
2. Don't wait till your friends can go with you, book your ticket now.
3. As spontaneous as you may be, planning to a certain degree is never a bad idea.

#23 You Are Not Alone

If at some point you feel as though you're just not getting a hang of this thing called life, you are not alone. Have you ever a met a full-on adult and realized… well, they definitely don't know what the heck they're doing? That's most of us. Even when we feel like we have it all figured out, there's always another level, another lesson and another experience for us to grow through. So, to feel alone in your problems at thirty, it's more like, welcome to the club.

Whether you're a single mom of three, a wife to a deployed marine, a "single status" hot mess who doesn't know what direction to focus in life, or an entrepreneur who has experienced success but still feels like something is missing. At thirty, you are thriving. If you are here, wanting to learn, grow, and invest in yourself, give yourself a pat on the back for making it this far my friend. There are so many of us in a multitude of different life situations, with life experiences as thick as an Iris Murdoch book and we are all on the same earth working to conquer and surpass our own distinct obstacles. Yes it can be intimidating but, you've got this!

I learned at a very young age that what makes us feel alone in these problems, is the fact that none of us are talking about it. Even more interesting, it's a proven fact, that if you get a group of women in the room, ask all of them to share their problems aloud and then give them the choice to take on someone else's life problems, the majority would rather stick to their own. I share this to say, we all have an imperfect life, with many labels we call problems. The notion of that level of humanness, should be a great reminder of how, in it together, we all actually are.

> " Everyone you meet is fighting
> a battle you know nothing
> about. Be kind. Always."
> -unknown-

I feel there's a certain strength involved in putting that smile on every day, even when you'd rather stay curled up in bed dwelling on worries of the future, scars from the past, or even a tough current situation. To me, there's an expiration date for those emotions. Feel them, yes. But know when it's time to step into your life again.

One of the most powerful things I've discovered is the value of connectivity. It's almost as powerful as the idea that something is unattainable or too hard to conquer, until it happens. The four minute run in the Olympics or surfing the grandest wave in Portugal; when we find and see others moving past their ideas of possible vs impossible, we too realize that we are more capable than we give ourselves credit for.

So if at some point you wake up in your thirties and feel all alone in your problems, you're not. Get that idea out of your mind. I know what it's like to feel so alone, that you wonder why you're here in the first place. Remind yourself, you are loved and valuable and this world needs you.

As an advocate for hiring professional therapists and seeking help, never feel like those things couldn't help you if you needed them to. But please don't let yourself stay down in the dumps when you have a beautiful life waiting for you to live.

I'm going to switch into some tough love here, something I wish I would have known sooner. There is no one that will knock on your door to check if the person you're dating is treating you how you deserve, or if you bought the perfect home before 29, had babies or froze your eggs, let alone if you established a four year university degree. All those things have been at the forefront of your thoughts in this time of life because of societal standards, please let them go. Now, I'm not here to argue what "the right way" is or that I hold any authority about it. What I am merely saying to you, is that you are far too amazing to keep beating yourself up over the standards you feel you have not met. It is you that will live with all your choices and also run the risk of regret in the ones you haven't made, but it's not to late to take action now.

All the problems that you currently have, the redirections from the things you thought you wanted most, it is all working for you but you have to search for the lessons in the pain. For now you must understand that the rest of your life is ahead of you. You have the potential to make anything you want to out of your life, and you can start now. It doesn't have to be in some grand way, like packing your bags to move across the country, or stop talking to everyone you feel is toxic in our life. Sometimes what strength looks like, is in the simplest of gestures, like standing there listening to your dad complain about life, while he tells you how to live yours, but actually hearing him out to understand him without judgments. To be so strong in yourself and your choices that nothing will sway you from your end goal, no matter how long it takes to get there.

But what to do with all the problems in between?

Well, there's no secret potion to mend that instantly. None of us have that magic pill to take it all away. We are all continuously unpacking different bricks of sadness, regret, loss, heartache, confusion, anger, disappointment, and they all weigh different on us. The bricks of sadness that you're carrying may be much heavier than mine, but I promise you wouldn't want to exchange that with the heavier amount of loss that I have felt and vice versa. We all have a story of the good, bad, ugly, and the incredible. So, why waste time trying to compare your losses or wins to mine. This life is no competition and this life isn't meant to be experienced alone. Life is far too precious to give up on ourselves and you are not alone in your pain; just remember that this too shall pass.

> " The heart that gives thanks is a happy
> one, for we cannot feel thankful
> and unhappy at the same time"
> -Douglas Wood-

What I wish I had known:

1. I'm really not the only person in this world, experiencing this one problem.
2. Everything really is Figureoutable (Thank you Marie Forleo) it just may not come exactly how you pictured.
3. Not even the worst days last forever.

#24 It's Time To Call Yourself Out On The Bs

I t's time to start eliminating the excuses and blame, for why you're not happy or where you want to be in life. If the story you're currently telling yourself goes anything like this, " It's because of them", or " "But it's not fair", " It's not my fault". I call BS.

Growing up, I almost couldn't imagine traveling out of state because it was just so expensive. How could I ever live a life of travel and wander with no more than a few hundred dollars in my bank account? I started imagining what life would be like if I only had the money to do it all. Then I realized that I didn't need to wait for a magic stork to drop a bag of money on my parents door step to have the opportunity. I would be able to travel and become a business woman one day because dang it, I felt like it's what I am meant to do in my life. It took sacrifice, discipline, patience and was really scary at times, but only because I didn't have the answers to my future. It wasn't enrolling into college and looking forward to the next four semesters of classes I could see planned out, then taking the adventure to push myself and survive it all. This... what I had decided, was standing on the edge of a cliff on a cloudy day, not knowing what was below me or if I'd catch just enough wind to fall. But I did it anyway, I followed what my soul compass was asking me to and the best thing I could have ever done was take a chance on myself.

There's being creative, bold and hardworking, and then there's this whole other level you need to reach to be so resourceful, that it impacts you in a major way. Being truly resourceful after all is looking for creative ways that you can leverage your current situation for maximum results and benefits. It's putting in the work and truly doing your homework for a lasting end goal that could change the course of your career and life. Here are a few ways you could become such.

#1 Only recently did I have a taste of financial freedom that allowed me to travel to over eight conferences in one year, all in completely different countries and states along with building and co-founding my very own conference. You know what I did before that, that I still incorporate till this day? I receive knowledge through the thousands of free podcasts, and YouTube videos that are out for you and I both to see. I shop at half priced book stores to make sure I have ready every single Dr. Wayne Dyer book that ever existed and I spend a tad bit more for local book signing engagements that will put me in a room full of women that I know have similar mindsets.

#2 Ask, Adapt, Apply. Because sometimes the only barrier between you and what you're wanting is a simple act of asking. Whether asking for an opportunity, collaboration, or mentorship. This doesn't mean you won't get no's or that it will make your end goal any easier to grasp, but the knowledge you'll acquire in the process can be priceless. Adapt by making challenges work to your advantage and lastly, apply all of your knowledge to each circumstance, because not everything should be done by textbook.

#3 Own up to it all. Stop blaming your parents, boyfriend, friends, boss. If you're in a bad situation, it's up to you to work your way out of it. Ask for help, talk to mentors, look for guidance from those who've gone before you. But make sure you don't end up living in victimhood and rather, step into the victor that you are. Owning up to all your mistakes, flaws, and insecurities, it gives you the strength to move on from them and into new opportunity. So with all the love, take the leap. You have it in your to create a better reality, if you're unhappy in your current one.

What I wish I had known:

1. Not coming from money and making that my excuse, is a cop out.

2. Just ask, you'll be surprised by the amount of yes's you will receive and where they will lead you.

3. The more honest you are with yourself, the sooner you'll tap into your greatness.

#25 Seek Respect, Not Attention

Time to strip off the masks, ladies. Literally, the face full of makeup masks that we sometimes hide behind. Btw, no shame if your makeup game is strong, I wish I knew all the things too. Where I'm going with this, is more the metaphorical route of the masks that we put on day in and out for the sake of feeling seen, relevant and liked. Yes, it's wonderful when we get attention from our teachers or mentors for our stellar performances, or our family for making them proud, our significant other or even from a complete stranger on IGTV. That is all good, and we are all human and love some attention, but when does it become negative though? Can seeking attention really turn life sideways? Like, wow, when did I stop recognizing myself?

First of all, our self-worth isn't correlated to the amount of likes, shares or thumbs up we receive on the daily, yet it still has the power to taint the perception we hold of ourselves. If there's one thing I'm so happy I learned at a young age, it was to seek respect and not attention. The bad attention that gets people looking at us for all the wrong reasons. Like, it's not enough to want to be real and show who we really are, but we now have to seem like we are being genuine, but with an edited body, face filter and background during a "candid" moment with five paragraphs of "hearth felt" commentary, some go as far as to turn authentic into spurious.

So, where's the line and how can we express our true authentic selves without getting swallowed by the big black hole that is the climb to a famous social status? Firstly, remember that people truly connect when you get past surface level. I'm not saying let's posts videos of us crying about every bad day or stop wearing makeup completely for the sake of authenticity. I'm saying that respect lasts longer because it is earned by the way you are contributing to this world. Therefore, that shift lies within the way you show up in the world and impact, not pure exterior appearance or lifestyle. You now have that admiration for showing up as your best self, while simultaneously growing through the same human mistakes half of the population has made. To under estimate the power of R-E-S-P-E-C-T is to ignore the real and raw, most beautiful qualities of yourself.

On top of the many reasons it's just ludicrous to try and be anything else but you, it's a lot more difficult to continue the act. Stay genuine, earn what you have and don't settle for less, than the love and respect you deserve because once you lose respect in yourself and cross that threshold, you also lose your confidence, charisma and then sense of self.

"Do not live for the temporary boost ups.
Live for the long lasting encouragements.
Only respect will give you that".
–unknown–

What I wish I had known:

1. The amount of acceptance for being yourself will astonish you, in a good way.
2. Filters are so much fun, but don't hide behind them.
3. Respect simply lasts longer than attention ever will.

#26 To: Boundaries, With Love.

O h, how I love to give. To give love and attention, to be there for people in times of need or to simply show that I am that friend, girlfriend, daughter, person that makes the effort to go above and beyond to show how much I care. To sprinkle so much darn happiness into your day, and not question of anything was left for myself.

Believe it or not, having unclear boundaries looks awfully similar to this and is disguised in many ways. It morphs into the shape of your best friend that keeps asking for your time and help with life, that when you suddenly say no, it could end a friendship. It puts on the beautiful mask of your lover and you wonder how you ever got so lucky. Yet at the same time, leaves you bewildered at why he or she has asked you for the fiftieth time to skip dance class to go do their thing instead.

It can be with work, family, relationships, friendships, your time, material things. Ladies, we are put to the test every single day with situations where we must set boundaries, with love. We can work on being our best self every single day, and yet the one hiccup that will cause that illusion of a stable foundation to crumble, will be the excuses we keep making for why we are going above and beyond our comfort and self-respect zone, for everyone else.

My hope is to share some pain points with you, that I discovered and practiced that has helped me. Here are the top five.

#1 EMOTIONAL- This includes emotional dumping from someone who is dismissing how you feel about certain situations or topics. Discussing things that you feel are inappropriate and/or make you uncomfortable should be verbalized. It may seem easier to pretend that things aren't a big deal, when they are. And you vocalizing such, will help saying no or drawing clear boundary lines, that much easier in everything else. Other times, those people who are crossing them, may not be aware of the effect their words or actions have. This is why it's up to you, to set those boundaries and then decide whether this person or situation is right for you thereafter.

#2 MATERIAL- We all work so hard for what we have. If someone is not valuing our belongings or treating them in a respectful manner, it is our duty to let them know where we draw the line. It's absolutely unacceptable to use or borrow a material possession and allow others to take advantage of this or make you feel obligated to lend, give or borrow your material things in the first place.

#3 PHYSICAL- Need I say more? Unwanted touching, whistling, public display of affection. Physical boundaries play major roles in our wellbeing as women. Especially with our lovers. We can be in an intimate relationship with our partner and kiss, touch etc… but we are not obligated to have sex, or do anything that makes us feel uncomfortable, goes against what we believe, or are just plain out, not in the mood to.

#4 TIME- The one thing we can never get back, is our invaluable time. We must start saying no more often, so we can give 100% to the yes's we decide to make.

This one also ties into the energy we give others. Our value of time is determined on the energy we provide them, such as a shoulder to cry on, the positive energy and insight we bring to a conversation. Be intentional with the time you choose to spend and with whom. If every time you leave the proximity of a specific person and find yourself drained, ask yourself if you've set a healthy boundary with the time and energy you're willing to give to them.

#5 MENTAL- This one is a massive factor in setting boundaries, especially because this one is mostly for yourself.

If you've ever put on your smiling face but inside you knew certain people, situations or things bother you and you're acting as if they don't... it's time to be honest with yourself. To have a better mindset, you must protect the energy that occupies your mind so that it does not drain you. If you're around people that do not give you the freedom to be yourself, that stand in the way of your beliefs and challenge your thoughts in a demeaning way, then reconsider what that could mean for your identity. When you have others taking up negative mental space, what room does that leave for positivity, creativity, and ways to experience those positive thoughts and emotions?

My hope is that one or all of these will resonate with you in some way, and you too are encouraged to set boundaries for yourself. Setting boundaries has become part of who I am and because so many new situations, people and conversations arise; I too, work to navigate this still. Just knowing I'm more self-aware of this, allows me to not place myself deeper in situations I don't want to be in. Doing such has taught me to not be afraid of being myself and to value my thoughts and perceptions of the world and people in it.

I've left some space below for you to write some of your very own. You don't have to come up with them all right now, but you'd be surprised how easy it is to list just a few ways in each category that you can integrate into our life. I encourage you to journal below about one way you can set a healthy boundary and brain dump, what that would look like for you. Think of people, conversations and situations you've been in that made you uncomfortable and do not want to repeat. How could you approach any situation that may be similar and incorporate your boundary setting? Sometimes, it's as easy as stepping away all together.

How will you set tangible boundaries in your life today?

EMOTIONAL:

_____
_____
_____
_____
_____

MATERIAL:

_____
_____
_____
_____
_____

PHYSICAL:

_____
_____
_____
_____
_____

TIME:

_____

_____

_____

_____

_____

MENTAL:

_____

_____

_____

_____

_____

What I wish I had known:

1. Setting boundaries is a form of self-love.
2. It's okay if your boundaries change as your relationships progress.
3. Always trust your gut feeling despite what your brain processes as logical. Sometimes you just know when something feels right or when it's off.

#27 Invest Wisely

What do you think of when someone says, make an investment?

Is it in stocks and bonds, on a new home or could they actually mean, in yourself?

The two types of investments I want to talk about here are about the investments we put into people; giving them our invaluable time and energy and then the financial investments we put into things like, school, careers, valued possessions and creative projects.

Before we start, list the last three major things you've invested in recently, be it money or time, within the last thirty days.

1. _____.
2. _____.
3. _____.

Now that you've done that, let's move on to a short story and we'll circle back around to those three things.

Between the two, my parents held three jobs and yet there were still days where the bills were barely paid at all. All I knew, was that when I grew up, I wanted to be financially sound and not be afraid that I'd have to put something back because I couldn't afford even the bare necessities. That's where my driving force to make and save money came from.

Whether your background came from financial struggle or not, that has nothing to do with why you can or cannot invest in your future. Nor does being attractive, popular, having 31.5k likes on social media have anything to do with the right ways to invest in yourself.

The key here is mindset and realizing your limiting beliefs, noticing the struggles that keep showing up in your life and then investing in a combination of ways that will help those particular areas.

As I've said before, your health is your wealth. In order to function at your highest level and continue showing up in all other areas of your life, your health has to take priority. Thus, being the one place I'd suggest you invest in first. So if you find that health is an area in which you struggle, then invest in a fitness/health coach to get you on the right path for your specific health issues and body type. Follow up with your physician even though it's not glamourous and may cost you and on the other, most important spectrum of health, seek out therapists, mentors or coaches that can help you improve your mental health and clarity.

Never be ashamed to ask for help when you need it, especially in seeking a therapist.

Maybe you're feeling lonely and you live in a small town, or you're living in such a huge city, you don't even know where to begin to make genuine friends. Invest your time and pay a small entry fee to a women's social. There's absolutely no shame in doing all of this solo, unless you make it such. The important thing here is that you join a community of likeminded people that are high vibe. People that are positively impacting you by simply being in that environment.

How about your finances?

Remember how I told you about growing up in very humble beginnings and that being my driving factor. Well, we all deserve to feel financially sound and free and to do so, it's important to be real with ourselves about where our money goes.

There's a quote I love that says, "show me your bank account and I'll show you where your priorities lie", and it's true. You can't tell me your health is important to you if all your money is spent on take out, cigarettes and other unhealthy things that are not positively fueling your body. Take it from a former smoker that quite cold turkey back in 2016.

We all have some type of vice and I'm not saying that any kind of change is simple but take one step at a time and make sure to make your priorities, your priority.

Lastly, something I teach and love to share is something I learned from an online mentor and thought leader. I've taken this advice and molded it into my own and it's this idea of investing in these four factors, that will help shape your life for the better.

It's paying attention to these four E's. Your Energy, Effort, Environment, and your Emotional Intelligence.

If you invest in your where you focus your energy, this will lead you to an optimal and positive environment; which is where you will physically place yourself and has a grander effect on your mood and outlook.

And just as you should be intentional about your energy, because as Tony Robins says, "Where your focus goes, energy flows", you should also be cognizant of the effort in which you put into everything you do. It's all connected and they're all investments that hold the truest ROI (return on investment), of your life.

Last but not least, to invest in the growth of your Emotional Intelligence is key. If you are capable of controlling the capacity in which you experience and express your emotions and are aware of the emotions of others, you will have found the key to both personal and professional success.

So my friends, Invest wisely.

What I wish I had known:

1. You don't need to give anyone an explanation of where you choose to invest your time, money, energy, or effort. You are the one that will live with the positive or negative outcome, so make sure you do what you know is right for you.
2. You shouldn't seek money advice from the broke, or wealth advice from the unhappy.
3. You don't have to impress people with things, the ones that are meant to stay in your life love you despite the material things.

#28 Face Your Feelings

Here's the thing, pretending you're not hurting will create unhealthy side effects just as dimming your light to make others feel more comfortable will.

The last few years, growing into someone I am proud to be and finally feeling like I am solid in my purpose, I still found myself dimming my shine because it made some people uncomfortable. It was an awkward feeling, because I finally felt " good enough" to show up for myself like, " Hey, I'm here and I am conquering this ride of life" but on the inside. On the outside, my mental shout was that of a, " Oh Hi, I'm Amber" in the softest of tones.

It had taken me so long to come out the other side. One too many years were spent apologizing for my dreams, saying sorry for my passions, and feeling bad for choosing work over hanging out, and I was done. I was over it.

I had lived too many years wondering, "Will I ever get this right"? When really, the better question was, am I following a path that I'm proud of. A path that resembles what my higher self-desires?

As many major life changes come, it took my whole world crashing down and burning into ashes to realize that hiding all my emotions was draining and destructive.

I began to learn the difference of knowing what the bright side looked like vs implementing those good thoughts and practices. So, I tried it. Within two full years, anger, resentment, sadness, grieving loss, I faced it and became more free than I had felt in a while.

After those few years, I felt so light and unbreakable until life slapped me in the face with some more heartbreak. Except this time, I was prepared. I wasn't bogged down from this mishap because that five lb brick, was one I refused to carry with me. It would have felt much heavier if I hadn't released all the other emotional weight from before, but this time I had learned and leaving that behind made the weight of this experience feasible.

Before we go further, I want to explain the definition of negative as it relates to our emotions. To be negative about something is a tendency to be downbeat, disagreeable, and always expect the worse. So, don't get this mixed up with being a negative person in general or that negativity is evil in all cases. Sometimes, being able to spot the negativity you're feeling can help you, because then you're able to pin point the cause of what switched your emotions.

You're able to identify things like your boundaries, the emotional connection with a person, place, or thing and you're able to have higher levels of self-awareness. So, how can you make sure your emotional response to the outside world isn't creating a negative loop of past traumas and bringing that into every current situation in your life? This is what I've learned so far from that and I'll sum it up in one long paragraph.

You will only learn about yourself and heal from your internal scars by facing your emotions. Know that we all come from different backgrounds, religions, social statuses and environments and within it all, the exact same opportunity or dilemma can enter your life the same way. This of course affects us all differently, and you don't get to choose how anyone but your own self should act when that happens, but it is vital to start from the beginning. If you don't heal past wounds from your childhood, teenage years, or recent adult years, how could you ever be ready for what's to come. For future arguments, disagreements, heartbreak, financial discipline or defining happiness when resentment, bitterness or anger still hold that space? That memory that you still have engraved in your mind that makes you feel like it defines you, when it doesn't. It starts there. Face your fears, call that person or don't, but decide to forgive them today, after all, forgiveness isn't for them. It's for you. Feel that pain all over again, from the person that broke your heart, then write a letter on why you're releasing them and burry it in the ground. However it looks for you, face your feelings and work to heal from them, so that you can experience the freedom and welcome in new, exuberant emotions.

What I wish I had known:

1. Opening up to people you love that love you, isn't weakness, it's strength.
2. Anger is easier to shift into, but still choose the ladder.
3. Give it to God, higher power, the universe. Whatever your beliefs, with this, you have the power to release any negative emotion that is causing pain within you.

#29 Your Age Doesn't Define Your Capability To Chase Your Dreams

Y ou know that moment when you look at a photo from just five years ago and think, wow, I used to be so fit. Then realize that the moment you took that photo, you felt fat and now want to slap yourself silly for ever feeling as though you were? Now, before you send me an angry email about body shaming, hear me out. Let's focus on the point. Your mindset may be the same way now, and I'm just trying to help you see that. Please don't wait five years before you realize how detrimental it is to act now, value where you are and save the excuses for never.

Just get up and do the thing. Face it till you make it, no faking necessary. Just like the last photo you found yourself reminiscing on, trying to imagine how you didn't see how wonderful you and your life was, you are better off now than you currently feel. You have so much more going for you than you realize and even if you feel you're in a bad season in life, it doesn't make it a bad life. You are 100% capable of pushing through this storm, just as you have every other storm that you faced in life and have survived till this point. It will be uncomfortable and scary. Maybe you'll have no support from your friends, spouse, boyfriend or girlfriend but this is all you!

Did you know, I was 21 years young when I felt like I was too old. It'd be easier to blame it on the world of modeling, but the truth is, I was impressionable and lacking both confidence and a growth mindset. I was so focused on my unattainable standard of beauty back then, that I missed how well I was actually doing for myself. I was traveling the world, signed with one of the world's top modeling agencies, I was in love, I made good money, all the things you feel would be enough, but they weren't. Nothing is enough, when your excuses are bigger than your gratitude and the reasons to morph into your best self.

It wasn't until I had built my second business and lost it all, that I realized, I had learned a thing or two about going all in on me.

It's too bad I felt too young when I started my first business. That feeling you get when you're in your twenties doing something major, yet your self-confidence is lacking because you swear everyone still sees you as just some kid, wearing higher heels than you're supposed to.

Imposter syndrome is real and wow, did it hit me hard. Granted, we all learn at different times in life and if you've never experienced that, well hey there Unicorn! Please write in and tell us the secret, it'll save us all a few years.

Just think of all the nonsense excuses we make for ourselves every time we want to go big. How many times have you failed before you even tried, because the negative thoughts floating in your head stopped you dead in your tracks, before your body even got up from bed? Think about the times you've hit snooze yet again, because how could you possibly start a healthy life now? You hate getting up early and you have a job that drains you, blah, blah, blah.

As much love as I want to give you here, I also want to help you help yourself. To help you expose the many truths you've buried or aren't paying attention to. To help you welcome change, because it's not that you can't handle the change you see in your mind. It's that you're not building the discipline consistently enough to make any change stick, thus leaving you in the same place you started.

You've got this. You've got this. You've got this!

I wish we could see ourselves the way our loved ones do, because they look at us with never ending potential. They see the ways we're capable when we lack enough confidence to see it in ourselves and they're the light we need to find within us.

So, from one former excuse maker to another; stop with the " I'm too old, It's too late to start" or the " I'm too young, they'll never take me serious", because that idea, dream and passion and love for whatever it is that keeps you up at night, it was put into your mind, heart and soul for a reason. I don't care if there are already ten million apps out there, if you have an idea for the next best one, you get on it. Whatever the thing is, that your life is asking you to step into right now, just drop the excuses of why you shouldn't and replace that with all the possibilities it can create in your life.

What I wish I had known:

1. All I had to do was own it! Every opportunity I didn't feel ready for, was just fear holding me back.
2. Stop waiting for the perfect time. It doesn't exist.
3. You'll only regret the chances you didn't take on yourself.

#30 You Will Lose Yourself

Nothing in this life is permanent, not even life itself. The good news is, neither are your failures or who you are in this very moment.

The beauty of this, is that we get to shape what exists.

Treat this moment as your masterpiece and sculpt it accordingly.

Maybe life seems so fragile right now and you're afraid of losing control? You've done everything you thought you were supposed to do to have a happy life, so why does happiness feel so far away? What truths have you been searching for and what have you discovered along the way?

Whatever path you're on, as in control as you feel, just release it. You will lose yourself. Now, before you go on thinking, "How dare you say that, I will never lose myself". Let me explain the beauty of losing yourself and why I believe it will happen time and time again.

Losing yourself isn't equal to losing your mind, direction in life, or validating that you're some lost soul never to be found. In fact, losing yourself has shown to be quite a rebirth of sorts.

Whatever you do, do not resist the organic change that may be happening for you now. That person you currently identify as, is someone that's been lost way before the moment you came into realizing it. Instead, give into what's happening and use it as a fresh start and a way to build yourself back up to an even better version of yourself. The 2.0 version.

I truly hope you don't imagine me as some teacher, pointing my finger saying, okay and now for this chapter, do xyz and everything will work out accordingly. I am not here to lecture you to say that any life or journey is easy or the same by any means. I'm not saying to take my word for it either, or that this process is convenient at all because as most of us know, change never happens at a convenient time in our lives. It's not enough that the relationship ended, but now your boss wants to fire you and some truck in front of you managed to pick up a rock that went flying onto your windshield from its tire, cracking it all the way down the center. Oh, yea... I'm sure it gets worse before it starts to get better. And as the saying go, "when it rains it pours". So please, if you're committing to this losing yourself process, know how far from comfortable it will be.

Also, sometimes losing yourself isn't a choice. Sometimes, life just begins to unravel, and you're left wondering, what will happen next? You wake up one day and it all hits you at once. The fleeting thoughts that get you anxious, the loss of energy, the wondering of what's next in life and that peculiar feeling that you can't quite grasp any of it at all. Not a single thing is making sense.

If you are feeling like you lost yourself, please consider this an opportunity. Let this be the time you allow this layer of learning and coping, as a chance to be better, wiser and more wonderful than ever.

Some people count these feelings off as being stuck, or in a bad season that seems to have lasted years. Don't let yourself fall away, don't stop living into your best life even when you feel disconnected from yourself.

Don't disappear into the darkness or allow yourself to sulk there for too long.

The beauty of these intense highs and lows you may experience is that it offers a clean slate of sorts. If you let it, it allows you to back track and find parts of yourself all while moving forward into the new habits and thoughts you will intentionally create. If you feel you have lost yourself, there is hope. Use the lessons this season has taught you and allow it to lead you thriving into your next chapter of life.

"Talk to yourself like you would
to someone you love"
— Brene Brown—

Now to begin finding yourself again.

This too will happen. You will find the strength. It may not happen for many sleepless nights, days of anguish or questioning of every action that you took to get to this point, but that day will come. That's why building your mental muscles are so important, because once you do this, getting back up from a sucker punch from life, will be much easier. You'll learn to cope, you'll know that life is full of tough things, but you're just as tough if not tougher and that this hard time, you will view as an opportunity to be the phoenix that you are, rising from the ashes.

After you have felt the lows and seeped into the downs that life seemed to have brought you to, you will wake up and decide that today, you will choose happiness.

You will take your power back and one day this hard time will be but a memory. The courage you will have built from that, will make you feel like the warrior princess that you are and you promise that it'll never happen again, until it does. In which case, the universe is only asking you to next level the life it knows you're meant to live into. So trust that.

You will lose yourself, but you will find yourself again, even stronger.

We can't escape all the hard things that we don't know are coming yet, but we can be our best selves now so that it never gets the best of us.

What I wish I had known:

1. Losing myself is just a call to action, to step into a better life for myself.
2. Getting back up will feel so good, so please don't stay down very long. You've got goals to crush.
3. Trust in divine timing. You may not be where you want, but someday you'll look back and see, that maybe it was just what you needed.

Amber Ybarra is an American Author, Entrepreneur, Podcast Host and Motivational Speaker. From former Elite signed model turned role model, Amber has founded The Positive Platform. Through this, she helps other female entrepreneurs reinvent themselves through high performance strategies for lasting change and growth in both lifestyle and business.

Amber resides in Texas with her precious four pawed daughter Zara and enjoys both domestic and international travel. Travel is what inspires her, as she values the exploration of different cultures and connections with people from all walks of life.

You can view more of her work, free tips on business strategies, mindset, and motivation at www.amberybarra.com. To listen in on her latest podcast episode tune into The Positive Platform Podcast and follow her journey @amberybarra.